Conscious Ascension

By Psychic Medium & Healing Channel

Judi Lynch

ISBN:069234442X
ISBN-13:9780692344422

DEDICATION

Dedicated to all the Lightworkers, Starseeds, and
Soul Travelers everywhere. You know who and what you are.
You Shine.

CONTENTS

Book Editing by Scott Taylor Lynch
Cover photo of Judi Lynch courtesy of Johnny Miller Photography

ACKNOWLEDGMENTS

This book is a collection of blogs, articles, stories and testimonies about the amazing power and incredible experiences of conscious ascension. For the last seven years I have been channeling, reading, learning, writing and doing my best to find the spiritual connections that heal to help us to evolve and ascend spiritually. After thousands of client readings, healing sessions, channeled messages and meditations, I thought I would write the sequel to my first book plus a little more.

Chapter 16 is my 1st book, Friends With Lights, A True Story, and it explains how I began communicating with a friend who had reached out from the consciousness after his death and how the experience changed my life forever. I rekindled how I had communicated with Spirit as a child and young adult. I asked for those gifts to be open to me again. It was an invitation.

Almost impossible for me to convey was the joy and elevation I was feeling those first few amazing and miraculous weeks. I was brimming with extreme vibrational energy. Others could feel it and my messages and healings were detailed, accurate and fantastic to say the least. I was ready but I wasn't ready for all the events that happened next. Why should I care what anyone else understands or believes in? I had witnesses to every event.

Even so, conscious ascension really isn't about me personally, it's about what I've discovered through my curious and questioning nature. I set out to prove something to myself right after my Dad crossed over almost 20 years ago. I had to know for myself that we never die and the energy of our spiritual consciousness lives forever. I didn't want to hear it from someone else, I wanted proof. I didn't even understand what ascension was in this day and age of information overload.

I've learned that miracles transform your life, but it doesn't mean everything will be flowers and sunshine. I know now that after a whole lot of joy, there are still a whole lot of life lessons still to be learned. As long as we are here, there always will be. Shine in that joy and keep it always in your heart. You will be tested and you will need it all through your life. The end result? Endless Love and Ultimate Healing!

i

1
STARSEEDS, LIGHTWORKERS, SOUL TRAVLERS AND MORE!

This is the first spiritual article I wrote and published in the Esoteric Library in 2007 and a couple of years later in OM Times Magazine;

They are here on a mission to heal and awaken and help raise this planet's vibration! Highly creative, self-motivated visionaries who are extremely sensitive to negative energies. Working in many different professions, they possess a light energy that make them fast healers and fast learners. They have the amazing ability to overcome any obstacle that would dare to stand in their way, tapped into the sources that help us to communicate, heal and learn. Plugged into the matrix and ascending faster all the time!

They go by many names and descriptions and practice methods of healing and communication once thought too "out there" by the mainstream public. Constantly updating their messages and their methods and sharing the evidence they possess that the Truth is indeed here! They have the ability to channel information and energy from places and planes existing outside the Earthly realm.

As we sort through the happenings and events and awakenings, we can see the progress! We can also see a larger divide between the awake and the sleeping. Pop culture can be a valuable tool for those who recognize the lightworkers scattered among the materialism, dullness and indifference. We can see the shining stars in the darkness and realize that there are obvious messages out there to help us "wake up!" A beautiful song, a breathtaking photo, a heartwarming movie, or an inspiring book can spark someone's fire to change their attitude and start looking into the Light!

Lightworkers are empathetic and sympathetic which make them vulnerable to others who may try to "steal" their energy. Paying close attention they soak up information like a sponge. Humble, but confident, sweet-natured and strong all at once. They live their lives expecting miracles because they know those miracles are possible. These are the souls who are dearly loved and deeply misunderstood at the same time. This is because the Earth has turned so gray in some places that other souls don't want to trust anyone or anything they deem too good to be true. This is changing! As thinking evolves and the Awakenings and Ascension continue, so will the understanding of the Lightworking Starseeds and Soul Travelers residing all over planet Earth at this very moment.

We are facing some of the biggest challenges ever right now and in the near future all over the World. Natural disasters are on the rise, many countries are in economic crisis, wars are still being waged and millions of children are in danger of starvation, disease and exploitation. Good souls are banding together and sharing their love and their knowledge to help in any way they can. Healers, psychics, writers, artists, poets, film makers and musicians are responding to the energy pouring in from the Heavens and answering the call. They are finding each other on the internet, through friends, networking everywhere they have the opportunity to get their work and their messages seen and heard!

As we move further into Ascension on this planet, the Lightworkers will be ready to help the world understand that there is hope living in us and all around us. The Earth will evolve and be reborn. There is a Healing Light Energy here like never before that continues to grow and shine. One will awaken another who will awaken another and another...

Judi's Notes: I wrote this in 2007, a year after I started channeling with my guides. Imagine my surprise when I started writing down messages about Ascension with details I actually had to verify online! Since I had never studied some of the information I began to write about, I had to know if it was correct. It was! At the time there were other people out there writing down the same things.

Judi, Tinki and Anni walking on the Appalachian Trail at Max Patch, North Carolina 2007. Photo by Scott Lynch.

2
SPIRIT GUIDE CONNECTIONS

Our Spirit Guides, beautiful souls who have most likely lived several lives on Earth in the past, now agreeing to help us evolve and ascend. They make a contract with us before our incarnation here to help us in our life journeys. They know our past and our life themes. They give us warnings and bring us comfort and healing.

Our guides communicate with us from the day we're born in several different ways, depending on our degree of ability to hear, see and feel their presence. Some people consider this "voice" to be their inner voice of consciousness but most likely it's their Spirit Guide they are hearing along with their built-in connection to Higher Realms. When a person's abilities are heightened, a guide's ability to communicate greatly increases, along with healing energy levels and the ability to heal the body and mind.

Children are often very able to hear their guide's warnings and also their laughter. Once I wrote down the name of a guide who was speaking to me for a woman whose reading I was about to do. I read it to her when she arrived and she told me that it was the same name she had given her doll as a child. I believe it was because she was able to hear her messages very clearly. It was pretty remarkable the information I received about this woman through her guide. That was probably because she was so psychically in-tune. She was also able to channel lots of energy, which I attribute to her being in Ascension mode. She said she could always feel and hear this presence around her but didn't know who to ask for help. It had frightened her for a long time before she started seeking out people who could answer her questions about the metaphysical and paranormal.

So how do we choose our guides and why do we make these "soul agreements" together for them to assist us here? Karma and past life situations are sometimes the key reasons we contract with certain souls. A soul who agrees to be a spiritual guide may also have special "soul knowledge" and resonate on a higher level which will be invaluable to the person's life themes and lessons.

Spirit Guides and Angels are very different in their missions here and vibrate at different energy levels but often they are working together in emergencies. Spirit Guides can seem much more Earthbound because they are working so closely with us, but Angels are much more advanced. Your guides can call on the Angels to assist when you may not be able to consciously do so.

Personally, I have found that the more I am connected to someone through friendship and spiritual readings, the more detailed information I get. For example, I was having a small workshop and someone's guide started giving me a dire warning about a situation. This man said he had no idea if this was true or not, it was the first he had heard of this "situation" going on behind his back. A few days later, I received a phone call from him verifying exactly what his guide had told me. It was really hard for him to believe that these people he had trusted would have done these things, but it was all true. I am used to people asking me questions and receiving clear and concise answers but when these warnings come in, it surprises me too.

Although our guides give us lots of insight and information to our lives, they cannot always interfere or give us exact instructions. They can help us to understand our options in life but they cannot always tell us which path to take. We still have our free will and other cosmic guidance that we can take into consideration. We are here to learn soul lessons and if it were that easy as having a guide telling you exactly what to do, well what would be the point?

Along with our Spirit Guides, we have Healing Guides who assist us by channeling energy when we are in physical, mental or emotional trauma. When I am giving a reading to someone, I almost always get information on the healing souls surrounding someone. These souls are often loved ones and friends who have crossed over who are assisting in times of crisis involving health and trauma. I have also been told that everyone is born with certain healing guides but many others join in later as they transition to the light.

I always recommend that anyone who wishes to channel energy and connect to their guides "protect" themselves with Ascension practices, meditation and prayer. These practices can help ensure that the only souls you are communicating with are there to assist you in this life. A person who practices Ascension Meditation and is tuning in will have the protection of legions of Light bearing souls! They have access to the knowledge of Saints and Ascended Masters and they love us dearly and unconditionally. We are all one.

(Published in OM Times Magazine)

Judi's Note: This is another article I wrote not long after I started connecting with my main spirit guide. He gave me his name, his story and a third eye vision of what he looked like. One day a friend said she could see him next to me. I didn't believe her. She said he was wearing a hat and sunglasses. I believed her after that. That is exactly the vision and description of himself that he gave to me from the beginning. I never told anyone. Would you?

In my readings for others, I always channel with the Spirit Guide speaking to me for that person. Normally, I start writing down things for someone after they make an appointment to see me. Before I ever meet or see them, the guide will come in and tell me things about them. Colors, thoughts, life themes, health information, etc. It is different for every person. Sometimes a loved one comes through before the reading begins. Most times they come through loud and clear when I am channeling during a session. I have found the more open someone is, the more energy there is for me to translate. I always get more information for someone who is at a higher vibration. I usually get much less information for someone who is in emotional turmoil or is unsure of their belief in the afterlife. I believe this happens because their spiritual energy is low. I make a bold statement when I say this; if someone says the medium isn't connecting for them, it may not be the medium's fault. We are all responsible for the energy we bring into the room, mistrust and negativity can absolutely be felt by an experienced intuitive. It can make a huge difference in the results of a reading.

3
THE MIRACLES IN THE MESSAGES

My experiences as a psychic medium/spirit guide channeler has taught me a lot about the soul and the reasons we are here beyond any book I could have ever studied. Every person is unique and every session brings new insight to me in the challenges people are facing in life. With each reading I ask that information will come through that can deliver miracles, hope and certain validation. I take great care to keep my energy strong and my channels clear and open. I also love to help someone else connect who wants to begin receiving messages and channel healing energy when they feel in pain be it physical or mental.

There have been times when I have wondered if anything would come through for someone who seemed determined not to believe in anything. I could even feel them blocking energy with their fear and negativity or unhappiness and depression. I found that in those times, it only made me more determined to help them understand that our souls are endless beings in human bodies. I have wanted for them to feel what I feel, to know that there is always hope and that we are never alone.

In the spring of 2006, my energy frequency increased dramatically. I received a page full of messages for my brand new next-door neighbor from her just recently deceased Mother. It was just as awesome for me as it was for her but it was scary too. I walked over with white roses in my hand from the rose bush in the yard and handed her the note. She read the note, sat down on the front step and put her hand over her mouth. She handed the note to her husband who read it looked up and said "How did you do that?" I had only met them once or twice or waved across the yard. I only knew that they moved from Florida, he was retired and her Mother had just passed on. I wrote down the names of people on the other side who had greeted her Mother when she passed and their personal messages to my neighbor. She told me just the other day that she sleeps with that note next to her bed each night and looks at it to remind her that they're in Heaven. Amazing! How wonderful is that for someone who needed this comfort.

One afternoon I was doing a reading for several members of one family who had lost a young husband and father. They did not want me to have any information about him to make sure it was really him who was coming through. The first thing he said was that his wheels had spun out of control. They said he was an auto racing fan and his messages went on and on until the validation was very clear, it was him. One woman wanted to know if I could communicate with her late husband. Among several things he told me was that he was holding out a lei for her and saying sorry. She said they were supposed to go to Hawaii but never made it before he died. He also told me several details about their life together and his personality, including whole conversations.

One afternoon I was doing a reading for several members of one family who had lost a young husband and father. They did not want me to have any information about him to make sure it was really him who was coming through. The first thing he said was that his wheels had spun out of control. They said he was an auto racing fan and his messages went on and on until the validation was very clear, it was him. One woman wanted to know if I could communicate with her late husband. Among several things he told me was that he was holding out a lei for her and saying sorry. She said they were supposed to go to Hawaii but never made it before he died. He also told me several details about their life together and his personality, including whole conversations.

When I have an appointment to see someone for a reading, most times I begin receiving information right away and start writing it down. I recall a particular time that a spirit guide came through and told me to write down a page of information for a woman who had emailed me for a reading. I laughed as I wrote down the colors black, baby blue, and a touch of pink. What the heck does that mean, I remember thinking. A few days later she walked in wearing a black track suit with a blue t-shirt underneath and pink lipstick. I handed her the piece of paper so she could see I had not written a thing yet and she laughed too. I didn't know what it meant when I wrote it but it sure was clear in that moment. She trusted me after that and I understood why I received those particular colors in my channeling. It was a great validation for her trust in the rest of the session.

One important thing I would really like to make clear about it all is that those of us who are channeling messages and energy have an important responsibility. We should be grateful to share the knowledge with others who want to do the same. Through belief, practice, meditation, good health habits and attitude, we can all become attuned to the energy to heal and communicate. I feel that we should always encourage a person to also tap in to their own guidance system and not rely on a spiritual advisor to guide every move they make in life.

We have to maintain our integrity. We have to understand there is a difference between those who have opened their spiritual gifts and those who want to believe they have. We are meant to bring each other hope and understanding and keep our egos in check. Channeled messages can bring validation but they can also help encourage someone to turn on their own portal to the light. We should never make someone dependent on us, but teach how these things are attained and maintained. That is the most important and beautiful thing about it, it can be shared.

We are pure light energy which has been increasing and evolving for many years. All the concepts are becoming form. All the impossible is becoming so. There is an energy which rides a wave we are meant to hear. In those energies, there are messages and healing, an in the healing, no fear. Miracles.

(Published in OM Times Magazine)

Photo By Judi Lynch 2011

4
THE INCREDIBLE POWER OF ENERGY HEALING

As we progress in our spiritual evolution by raising our vibrational energy levels, we discover something quite miraculous. The incredible power of energy healing on the body, mind and spirit is increasing at a rapid rate. We are practicing the concepts that bring us the knowledge to spark our brains into action. Through this insight we are truly progressing and moving forward. More people are discovering the ability to channel themselves to good health and spiritual wellness.

Through countless methods and modalities, activation has accelerated and the channeling connections are being made. The etheric energy surround our bodies is responding to our requests and we are taking better care of ourselves. We know that what we put into our bodies and minds matter and we have combined our good intentions to manifest miraculous healings. Healing the body of once thought incurable disease with the power of our thoughts! Conquering depression and anxiety with the touch of energy from Heaven bringing back the joyous thoughts we were all born to experience. Our cells are responding to our thoughts and leaving behind that which was once inherited by family biology and unchangeable.

All over the World for centuries, humans have practiced many forms of spirituality and holistic healing. Many times this culture and knowledge was lost over the need to control the forces of energy being channeled and govern the information coming in by those who wanted all the power for themselves. We can compare this with our modern day situations. We have witnessed how the need for material things and financial gain has corrupted people. They became filled with greed and the need to control. There is no other way for man to learn but to experience. We have been building this house of ascension since we first came here. The difference now is that we have more knowledge and better tools!

We have now evolved to the point of or proving we can change our human biology by transmuting our thoughts to the etheric level. We are creating the mental particles that manifest into healing light energy that lifts our physical bodies into the next dimension; this is changing our very cell structure! Metaphysical Science of the most inspiring kind is knocking at everyone's door. More people are walking through that door every day. Changing their minds about why we are here, wanting to know the reasons why, and wanting to feel that energy which brings in that healing light. Every time that happens, the collective energy of every one is raised by one more energy field of light adding to the vibration. Truly amazing!

If you have ever been in a room full of spiritually minded people praying and asking for healing, you have no doubt felt, heard or seen this energy coming through in a magnified force. It is an experience that stays with you forever. It would stand to reason also that not only do we each have our own body chemistry but we also have our own spiritual chemistry. An idea for one person may not make sense, but for another, their way of meditation and spiritual connection complete a connection for them and helps them to ultimately heal from anything. It can be an instant healing or take several years. It is happening because our consciousness is letting it in.

We were born to have hope, a reason to be here, to understand more and now we are responding. Our mental perceptions of the Other Side and the Universe are coming into focus. Our senses are waking up to every possibility available to us through our endless creations in light and love.

(Published in OM Times Magazine)

5
MEDITATING WITH YOUR SPIRIT GUIDES

Many people have challenges with the concept of meditation and just exactly what it means. They want to understand how to attain that beautiful state of peaceful bliss. For those practicing advanced spirituality, meditation helps them to strengthen the connection to their source energy. The guides, ascended masters and angels who help convey knowledge, insight and healing heed to this connection. While in a high vibrational state of meditation, you are completely able to control the physical body with the spiritual body and be conscious of it; thereby training your mind to stay in this state while awake. Your body can be in a constant state of renewal and recharge if you are channeling in higher realms during meditation.

The first thing to realize is it is your state of mind and not your location that matter. Some people can meditate and connect in the middle of a crowded and noisy room. They can also zoom in on people and situations going on before anyone else notices a thing. Others are too distracted by every noise and movement in the room to be able to maintain the focus they need.

Your own personal spirit guides surround you at all times with their vibrational energy. When you tap into this stream of spiritual light, their light becomes one within you, and combined with the energy from the Source, it heals our every need. This is the energy of miracles. This amazing force calls upon the Angels. They can hear our prayers, answer our calls to be healed, and lifted up into the vibration of joy and absolute peace. This is the peace all of us long to feel as soon as we are born here. This is the spiritual consciousness that thrives in us and connects us all.

The light which radiated from us when we came here, that we think we might have lost sometimes, is only a prayer, a vision, or a thought away. The ability to call on the souls in the consciousness who love us fearlessly and unconditionally is the super power of pure love which created us to which we will always return to.

As you become accustomed to the energy and the light your guides are bringing in with them, you will start discovering your own unique abilities to communicate. It takes courage and practice. There are many signs of awakening you can experience and build on to strengthen your bond with the souls who are there to assist you from the light. You may be able to feel a presence, a blast of air, a touch on your forehead or hear a bell ring. All of these signs are telling you that your meditations are successful.

Each of us may have our own ways of connecting in our prayers and meditations. There are no rules. If Spirit is coming through to you and healing your needs and comforting your fears, where and how you connect makes no difference. Whether you are standing at the top of a mountain looking out a beautiful valley or kneeling in a great cathedral, just know you are worthy of the love you are receiving.

(Published in OM Times Magazine)

6
SHINING YOUR OWN LIGHT

"Never let anyone steal your thunder." Most of us have heard this phrase several times during our lives. We understand what it means intellectually but we might not always recognize it when it's happening. It might just sneak up on us and before we realize it, we have forgotten to shield ourselves from the negativity which ignites our fears to strip away our confidence.

We are living beings of pure energy and we thrive on light and positive thoughts! When another soul comes along and does or says something hurtful, it is always your attitude and your reaction which determine its effect on you. If you are living from a place of love and spiritual maturity, it is much easier to process and forgive. We have our own energy source available to us at any time and we never have to rely on others for that source. We also have to protect it from those who would consciously or unconsciously try to draw it from us when their supply is low instead of receiving it from within.

Since everyone is at their own level of mastering their spiritual consciousness, we learn to be patient, without judging as we realize we all have our roles to play and our challenges to heal.

We currently live in a society that thrives on judging each other constantly; it can be very confusing to live with this concept when you are trying your best to spiritually evolve.

When we learn to master our negative thoughts and reactions, we unveil an emotional freedom that transcends the control dramas and situations which dim our light. It is a process of changing the way you think about what you have experienced and removing yourself from expectations. Accepting the situation exactly as it is. The acceptance gives clarity to the reasons why the experience was given to us in the first place. We learn to remove our selfish ego thoughts and step back to see the miracle of the lesson. Many of us have to unlearn the things we witnessed growing up within our own families. It takes practice for us to stop reacting to the triggers which make our ego react to negativity. Once it becomes clear to us that our actions are actually feeding the situation, we can choose to feed it with positive light and requests for healing.

You regain your inner power when you free yourself from co-dependency and blame. Your confidence can never be shaken when you identify within yourself that you are unconditionally loved and you need no other human to supply that love. This emotional freedom also gives us the insight and the means to advance spiritually, therefore raising our vibrational energy to heal our every need. Body, mind and spirit can feel the release it brings! The weight that is lifted from the heart by giving understanding and forgiveness to others is amazing!

If we can all learn to love unconditionally, there is love enough to heal everything. We might have to keep reminding ourselves when someone commits a horrible crime; they are playing out a karmic drama. We have no control over the soul lessons agreed upon by those involved in the situation but we can certainly send our love and prayers to heal it. We create the atmosphere to choose our reactions and how we act upon removing ourselves from dangerous and hurtful situations as well. It is up to us to recognize when we need to act to diffuse a negative outcome. Sending more negativity to a situation with gossip and revenge only creates more drama and negativity but sending out healing light energy creates a beacon of hope that things will turn out okay. There is a difference between karmic justice and ego centered revenge. The Universe will take care of it if we can just let it go out to the consciousness and back again. Release equals the manifestation of miracles.

It is truly up to us to be responsible for shining our own light. Others like you will recognize it and be on the way to enhance yours for everyone around you collectively to shine your lights together. So put up your light shields and shine from the inside. Keep the knowledge that your light can never dim without your permission. You are the master of the flame where Source resides inside you.

Healing Light Meditation

As you meditate upon your God self, you magnify the energy in your soul. Mastering any negativity, you visualize unlimited potential. Body, mind and spirit can heal anything through this pure white light energy.

Your being is radiant with light. See your own face, perfected and sublime, in this field of light and visualize it streaming down from 18 feet over your head, its ray's extended down over your entire aura.

This Healing light energy is now streaming from above through your crown chakra and down through every chakra and cell in your entire body. Every atom of your being is radiating light. Breathing in this beautiful light and feel it's ultimate healing and joy.

You are filled with non-judgmental peace and well being. You have returned to the light that gave you life. There is your inner self that knows you are loved and protected in all ways. You have the light within you at all times. You are healing. Pure light and love have healed you. Your guides surround you holding you in their light energy as long as you need to be there. When you open your eyes, you are healed with this energy and your life force has been renewed...

Return all emotions to peace, to the balance point. Trust God, not as an outside force but as a force that lives inside you endlessly waiting for the streaming healing light to assist your every need. Within you there are miracles waiting to happen...

(Unpublished, taken from Judi's online blog)

The Barn Orb, Keel Mountain, Alabama 2007. Photo by Judi Lynch

7
FINDING OUR SOUL FAMILIES

Where have you been? I've been looking for you all my life and I didn't even know it! The familiar soul you meet one day you swear you know from somewhere but never met in this lifetime. It has probably happened many times during your life, this soul deja vu. You meet someone who resonates with your very heart and you wonder how the Universe helped you walk right into each other's life.

In this age of rapidly accelerating energy and evolutionary ascension, we are experiencing this soul recognition more frequently than ever before. Many of us are finding our soul families online. The world becomes a different place as we understand that we have to take more responsibility for our personal environment. Many of us have been on the quest of surrounding ourselves with "light" minded people. It has become so much easier for us to explore and communicate with each other. It gives reason and a higher meaning to the technology explosion we have had to adjust to in just the last few years. It becomes obvious that without it, we could never have come together spiritually in such a remarkable way.

Your soul family can be more than just other people who think like you do. They could have incarnated with you through different lifetimes throughout the history of the Earth and beyond. They are your cosmic sisters and brothers from the Other Side. You may have once lived in a colony together and made a pact to find each other in this or that life. Depending on your life choices and ability to listen to the signs and messages, you may realize this phenomenon several times. You will feel instant recognition and understand many things in common between you. You know what the other is thinking without saying a word. You have the same spiritual beliefs and questions. You feel energy between you that is on another level. You know this person was truly in your life chart to assist you and you them. You can also possess a very strong psychic bond and share healing energy that is very advanced.

Have you ever felt the family you were born into comes from another planet? Your ideas and personalities may clash in such a manner you wonder if we all really do choose our blood family before we incarnate. You may feel that you never belonged with or been understood by the very people who gave you physical life and most of the immediate family around them.

Consider (remember) that this dynamic may have been exactly what you needed to raise your vibrational energy field by completing your soul theme challenges in this life.

The control dramas and life scenarios played out between you, no matter how absurd, have assisted in the soul growth you needed to spiritually evolve. We all eventually come to realize holding on to these painfully difficult family situations hold us back from completing our life themes and healing the past. It may be absolutely necessary to remove yourself physically from this kind of constant negativity to heal emotionally and spiritually. You can still forgive and move on without having to ever be in the same space again. Some of the loveliest people on Earth have been raised in cruel and heartless circumstances. They somehow know that they are on a higher vibration and they keep moving forward to a higher purpose. You can always free yourself to recognize your true soul family! It is genuinely possible to find peace and harmony within that helps your purpose shine with others.

Millions of people who are thinking the same thoughts, getting the same messages, and awakening the new era have started sharing and creating miracles together in a very short time. Collectively we understand each other. Members of your "soul family" will weave their way throughout your lifetime. Your level of awareness, combined with theirs, can spark miracles of recognition, healing, and fantastic events! Where have you been?

(Published in OM Times Magazine)

Judi Lynch, Crystal Healing Spiritual Center , 2008. Photo by Scott Lynch.

8
ARE YOU LIVING WITH GHOSTS?

There is more than one way you might be living with ghosts in your life. We all have shadows and perceptions of a place that exists where things seem hollow, gray and empty. It is a place where everything seems frozen in time, without resolve, growth or change. This is where ghosts of every kind can take up residence without paying rent! They can block the light energy that is constantly available to you, making you dim your own light in response.

When we hold onto the past for too long without letting go, we risk being haunted by our memories. It is the same as cleaning the house. We have to sweep out our minds and our hearts to be able to hear what our spiritual guidance is telling us. When we open up the channels with good intent and a compassionate heart, we call on all the spiritual guidance available to every soul.

Why are there ghosts walking among us here on Earth? Bound by the past, they can not see beyond the darkness or feel the light. We emulate that behavior here when we let ourselves become frozen and stagnant, afraid to move. Our fear takes over good sense and spiritual reality. We create the situation to give us an excuse. Sooner or later, we have to admit we are responsible for our own light. We have to pick up the broom and learn how to forgive, let go and move on.

Free yourself from the echoes of the past. Rewire your heart and mind to only accept the good and positive things about yourself to nurture. Learn how to heal from all the harsh words and judgments from yourself and others by filling your heart with compassion for those who have pain inside. We aren't meant to take away their pain by letting their words discourage us, we are meant to help lift them up. Everyone is just now finding out how our vibrational energy matters. Some people are still figuring out how responsible they really are for their ability to feel joy and radiate light. It is liberating and a little scary at the same time. It takes time to get used to.

The ghosts who live among us are much like the ghosts of past lives and thought created energies. We have the ability to send them all into the light for healing. Visualize the total transformation of a lost soul asking for direction. Needing to know nothing more but that there is no force greater than the unconditional love waiting for them. See yourself in that same unconditional love force. You are totally forgiven, totally healed.

There is a radiant place for each one of us to discover inside when we ascend our thoughts. There is a healing light shining in every corner of this planet. Whether you participate or not, it will always be there. When you're ready to receive it, you'll know. A spark will get you there and grow into a fire of understanding and knowledge. Nothing is ever lost or without reason. Everything is a lesson, whether it is a lesson in joy or pain. It is a beautiful release to witness when the ghosts disappear and the light comes streaming in.

(Published in OM Times Magazine)

9
THE ELEVATION OF YOUR VIBRATION

We are discovering more fascinating and miraculous proof everyday that we are ascending at a more rapid pace than ever before in our history here on Earth. Energy grids around the World are pulsing with healing light energy. We only have to learn how to hold this amazing energy in our very hearts to understand its incredible power to heal every part of us.

Awakening to new possibilities in our abilities to communicate and channel these energies into realities, we are able to visualize healing ourselves, each other, and this planet together in an amazing collaboration. We can encounter a true realization that the answers are in our beliefs and our beliefs are the answers. What you create truly and incredibly become reality. Whatever negativity you leave behind helps to raise your spiritual consciousness into levels you have never before touched as a soul.

How do we take full advantage of the gifts we are blessed with to grow and nurture? How do we raise our energy vibrations in such a constantly changing environment? It can seem like a huge task to those who are still struggling with certain concepts. Any negative feeling or situation that you hold onto in this life or from a past life stays with you and on through the next reincarnation until it is healed. Purging egoistic thought is imperative to the amount of vibrational energy you are able to hold and channel. You start creating positive light energy the moment you release all that holds you back!

When you are aligning the ego with the soul, every decision you make can either help to fill you with light and confidence or send you right back to deal with the same life situation yet again. We choose to either serve the ego self or validate our spiritual consciousness with unselfishness and devotion. Your consciousness and your ego work together to work out the individual soul themes we are all working on. It can take great courage to learn to forgive others in difficult circumstances, but that forgiveness brings about an explosion of beautiful miracles. This kind of growth is priceless for the soul and grows without expectations of reward. It represents a soul theme realized, understood and healed.

Meditating on the soul chakra will help in your attunement to the new energies being offered. The soul chakra connects your awareness to the God source and is your safe place when you encounter a spiritual battle within. We can reach up and out into the consciousness to access glorious visions and information that calm us with remarkable peace and understanding. It is contained in the light energy particles that each of us is a part of and we only need to awaken that part of us which knows this to experience tremendous growth. Whatever makes our essence lighter lifts us up to the next level of energy and beyond to the destiny of our true purpose and form.

(Published in OM Times Magazine)

10
SPIRITUAL CHALLENGES

In this amazing time of heightened awareness and new thought spirituality, we all have some unique challenges ahead. This age of ascension has changed everything! We are individuals on our own unique soul quests, working towards a collective energy of oneness in the Universe. These growing pains are a big part of our spiritual self-mastery as light beings in these evolving human bodies.

We are all learning to take better care of ourselves; Mind, Body and Spirit. We learn by living, feeling and asking questions. Those who have raised their vibration through soul development have to be cautious with their ego. Humility plays an important part when teaching others who have asked for assistance in their own personal challenges. Everyone has their own soul history, themes and lessons to learn and accomplish. Respecting and honoring this in everyone will save a lot of frustration and hurtful situations of every trying to "make" someone believe in everything that you do.

We also have to remember that we will still be tested no matter what obstacles we might have faced in the past. The incredible joy that we are able to feel through our spiritual connections will always be there but in these human lives, it ebbs and flows. We have to realize that we are not immune to future catastrophic events but we are much better equipped to handle them through our knowledge.

Many people try to practice spiritual technique without being able to work out ordinary human problems. They are unable to do the soul mastery work needed to raise their vibrational energy and don't understand what they are doing wrong. They are spiritually gifted but their soul is left with unaccomplished themes, they feel disappointed inside. They sometimes resist feeling human emotion and hide from confrontation when this is exactly what they really needed to heal.

Remembering to practice trust in the Universe is also very important. How do we gain trust that everything is for a reason and in the end it will be okay? By walking through fire successfully and overcoming fear. We also have to learn to balance common sense with spiritual matters. Building our consciousness collectively makes use of the higher energies needed to accomplish miracles in our lives. Have faith that doing the "soul work" matters. Practicing forgiveness, patience, compassion and courage all assist to balance the ego. This helps the process of channeling the pure light energy we are all part of.

We are never alone in our challenges and quests in these Earthly lives. We have to forgive and be kind to ourselves when we feel we have failed somehow. What we may consciously think of as a setback or failure is part of the process as we are still learning how to transmute light and positivity from negative situations. When we release the negative emotions and thoughts we may have gathered through the years, we lift not only our own vibration but everyone else's around us as well. As we let go and live in the now, knowing the future already shines, we illuminate our souls!

(Published in OM Times Magazine)

11
THE MAGIC IN A MYSTICAL MIND

What exactly is the mystical mind? Is it so much different from the normal way we have been programmed to think as humans? What is different about those who possess the metaphysical skills to heal with energy and to read and transfer thoughts telepathically that makes them able to operate on such magical terms?

The answers can be hidden in the way we evolve our thought process as we mature. In the heart of a small innocent child, anything is possible. The imagination can be endless, boundless and timeless! Life can seem to be one surreal adventure after another. As time goes on, the child has to learn to live in the reality of the society they live in and conform to the popular thought process. A child learns that there can be certain consequences to "strange" behavior.

Although it might seem the opposite, this logical thought process and intellect are absolutely necessary in order to evolve us all into a state of higher consciousness. These thoughts evolve into questions and more questions. A mind that turns from being childlike and mysterious to stagnant and grey will just accept whatever they are told. A mind that questions, educates and experiences learns they can conjure up questions that have never been asked or answered before. This is where mystical magical thinking creates miracles! The combination of the thought process that accepts both rationally and joyfully is the ascending mind!

Just because someone has intuitive ability or can feel or channel energy does not automatically mean they know how to manifest anything they desire. They may not even understand their abilities at all and use them on a daily basis. Where magic comes into play is when they "wake up" spiritually and are consciously aware of the power of thought and manifestation. Wow! It may take only a word or an action from someone else and it can ignite a light that heals and inspires thousands of others to do the same. Compassion, forgiveness, non-judgment, encouragement, understanding, acceptance; these are the concrete concepts for now and for our future here.

The energies of the ascension are here and getting stronger. We have the ability to channel away the hurt, pain and negativity that holds us back. There is a love filled with glorious light and healing in these incredible miraculous vibrations and we are now learning to hold those vibrations at the highest level. Filling ourselves with the peace of mind that is being offered to us now, this is how it was meant to be.

When we consciously and collectively learn not to accept the negative thoughts that destroy, we will create more thoughts that heal, nurture and grow our spiritual selves. How simple it should be that by changing our minds to only know love, we evolve the soul of the heart for everyone and everything. Expanding the love we feel for ourselves and others leaves no room for anything else to penetrate. It heals us with astounding completeness. Healing every human on Earth would light up this Universe so brightly, that those in the next might come by to say hello more often. Isn't that an amazing thought?

(Published in OM Times Magazine)

12
THE EMPOWERED SOUL

We go through our lives making countless choices and decisions. Some of them will turn out to be fantastic and some of them may be great and painful lessons. It is in the processing and action we also decide how we grow or if we choose to remain stagnant and unchanging in our view of the world. How is it that some people never find their way out from great tragedy and depression but others seem to have a greater understanding of the meaning of life and our "soul missions?" It is desirable for some souls to keep focused in spiritual ritual while others are more served by their own unique spiritual path to keep seeking more knowledge.

An empowered soul is capable of manifesting the future that best resonates with their awareness of it. They are "awake" inside the consciousness that resides in us all in a more connected, higher vibrational plane that is materializing in the physical realm. This process has been sped up in many and is continuing to spiral into more and more "awakenings" every day. We will continue to see more people seeking outside assistance to get through their daily lives as this process of ascension continues. Anxiety, fear of the future, and the unknown are the main reasons people seek assistance through alternative healing. Not everyone will want to participate and that's okay, too. They will still be a part of the plan and a part of the love that connects us as one.

We are all discovering how to empower ourselves with knowledge and inspiration. In other words, the keys to the ascension are being discovered as we evolve our consciousness. Fear is keeping many from turning the lock to open the door. It takes courage to go beyond the basic reality of what you have been taught your whole life. The concepts that no longer make sense can really bring on anxiety if you are in an environment still operating in an old system of belief you no longer agree with. The symptoms of a collective fear are growing among people who have lost hope. This is obvious to see among the events taking place right now, but the Light inside those who are awake is getting brighter all the time.

We are all responsible to empower ourselves with our own truths and different ways to shine without judgment. We are losing the excuses to be in pain or fear over the past and what is to come. The spiritual help is out there now. We also have more knowledge than ever before of how to take better care of ourselves body and spirit. If we have the courage to reach out for more understanding, to devote the time and energy to elevate our being, we can bring light to any situation this world can face. Universally, we are reaching out and finding out we really can communicate and touch energy is a way that has never been felt before. How can it not be both an extremely joyous and completely frightening at the same time? It is in the understanding of what it means to be attuned to the Light that heals us and to understand how amazing that really is. The power it conveys to us is a miraculous gift! Together we are radiant.

Doreen Virtue: "Anything that you fight with or struggle against grows larger. You give power to lower energies by focusing upon them. You don't eliminate darkness by arguing with it. The only way to eliminate darkness is to turn on a light."

(Published in OM Times Magazine)

13
TRAVELING ON THE ASTRAL PLANE

You don't need to pack a suitcase or make a formal reservation. We can all travel without the wheel or the engine. Our intentions, thoughts and emotions can be felt in an instant. It has always been possible in our evolution to discover this but a little challenging to control. It takes courage, knowledge and practice; bi-locating to remote view, comfort a loved one, or save a life is happening more every day on Earth.

We have an astral body that vibrates at a higher frequency than our physical bodies, with it we explore realms and dimensions we have only imagined in our human form. The astral body looks just like us but it is not as solid and dense. Every sense is heightened and psychic ability pours in through the phenomena of this higher vibrational energy.

We're most likely to astral travel when we are sound asleep and physically unaware. Do you have dreams of flying? Have you every sat up in bed in the morning with a complete feeling of euphoria and purpose but you aren't sure where these feelings came from. You have the most amazing crew of spiritual beings, loved ones and spirit guides helping you! Whether you are aware of them in your waking hours or not, they can work miracles while you sleep. All you have to do is ask and the energy to lift you up will be there.

Our loved ones, who have crossed over, astral travel across dimensions to lend their love and endless reassurance of the healing light available. Now, more than ever, it is being experienced in all ways! Mentally, physically and emotionally, the astral travelers are coming into our consciousness and enveloping us with all the ability available to us to heal. We are all still learning how to let the light come streaming in after all we have been through to find our way. To touch, feel and know the other side of life is really there brings about the most amazing transformation you will ever know!

I personally remember several profound paranormal events as a child where I knew something very remarkable had taken place, although I could not explain it. One afternoon in third grade I put my head on my desk during break time. I remember really wanting to be on the play ground where the other class was laughing and playing outside. In an instant I was standing out there watching everyone when I saw my best friend fall down and scrape her knee. After school she showed me the bandage from the nurse's office. I told her I had seen the whole thing with my 'other eyes' while I was taking a nap.

Another time I was playing in my front yard when a man appeared in front of me with blood on his head. He said he had been in a car accident and needed help. I ran inside the house to tell my mom but when we returned to the front yard, no one was there. Later we discovered there had been a car accident on the road going past our subdivision and this man had been found unconscious but alive in the ditch that afternoon. He had a head injury from the accident. There is no way he could have walked to our house; he had never physically left the crash site.

A psychic is able to see into and read etheric energy through the consciousness because they experience everything on a higher vibration. Every sense is heightened, bringing in messages from guides, pulsing, vibrating light energy, knowledge from ascended masters. It is really true that the more we can release emotionally, the lighter we become. Our souls can shed all the struggles and heal from past emotion through astral travel. As we learn to use the skills that come with this incredible light energy of the ascension, we will shine a light on each other like never before. We will all become astral travelers, healing together as one. The journeys are endless and the scenery is breathtaking!

(Published in OM Times Magazine)

PART TWO

EXPERIENCES, TESTIMONIES & HEALING MIRACLES

14
MESSAGES FROM THE FUTURE

When I started channeling energy and receiving messages in 2006 I wrote down several soul messages from friends and family. Some of them were from the future! Since time does not exist on the Other Side as it does here, I could not discern the difference. Two people came in from my childhood and teenage years who told me they had passed, also how they passed. Only it hadn't happened yet!

I was told my friend Dean had a severe heart problem and he had sent me a message from beyond that he should have taken better care of himself. I was also told my friend Steve had died way too soon at home suddenly and that he had a wife and children. I had no way to validate this information at the time about either of them.

I had seen Dean about five years before that but I had not seen Steve since I was about 17. He was a couple of years ahead of me in school, had joined the army after his graduation, and his family had moved away from the area.

Imagine my shock when Dean emailed me and sent his phone number one day about a year later. Sure, we'll be at the party, I replied. When I saw him he looked really bad. He was pale, swollen and tired. I asked him if he had been having chest pains or pain in his arm. He said yes, I haven't been feeling well for awhile. I told him what I was doing for a living now and he had to get to the doctor immediately or I was going to call his sister. A couple of months later he called and he told me they had diagnosed him with severe blockage in his heart arteries plus put him on medication to break up the plaque. He jokingly said, "Thanks a lot, Judi! Now I have to take this $%^& medicine for the rest of my life."

A couple of years later I noticed a friend from school on my Facebook page that might know where my friend Steve was now. I told him if he ever heard from him, to tell him I said hello. Maybe my premonition on this was similar to Dean's situation. Maybe it had already happened and Steve had crossed over. I had no idea where he had moved to. His name was very common and it was not easy to check so I let the Universe decide if we would ever be in contact again. Somehow though, I felt that we would. On this side, the other, or both.

In 2013 I received my answers and my validation. Steve sent me a friend request. He was still alive. He posted a birthday greeting on my page in July and I thanked him. In mid-October I noticed my friend count had gone down by one. He was missing from my friends list. I was too afraid to look. Maybe he had taken down the profile. So I waited. After a few weeks, I looked up his name. His obituary said he died in October, 2013 suddenly from a short illness. It made me so sad to think we never got to speak to each other again but I was happy to know we said hello online and saw each other as adults. I was very grateful for that but I was trying to understand why I didn't reach out sooner and say something. The answer is it wouldn't have mattered. The answer was we had closure in this lifetime, he felt what that means.

Many years ago, before I started doing spiritual work, I received an incredibly profound message and premonition at the same time. It filled me with anxiety for months. It was Spring and I sitting in the back sear of a friend's car with my husband on our way to play mini-golf. A warning came through to me of a car accident. I distinctly heard my guides tell me to never ride in the car with this person again, and to tell my husband to politely offer to drive us all in the future. They laughed at me of course but to me it was so loud and strong I could not forget it. A few months later, he called and invited my husband (who declined) to a football game. On the way to pick up the tickets the morning of the game, our friend was killed instantly at a railroad crossing. He had just come back from morning Mass at church and he stopped by his parents to get the tickets on his way in to the city. It was hard to believe, he wasn't even 30 yet. My husband said he would believe me from now on. If I got a warning, he wanted to know.

I remember meeting people, knowing what would happen to them, but not understanding why I was supposed to know. I realized it helped to keep me alive and questioning fate. It is incredible to me the number of people I have known throughout my life who seem to have left the earthly plane way too soon. When I was eight, my best friend in the neighborhood lost her mother (also in a train accident) and I could not imagine how she must have felt as a child. I could see her Soul. I could actually see her mother floating about three feet above me after the accident, but I was too young to understand it wasn't a normal thing to see.

15
FROM THE HEART

Over the years I have received thousands of emails, letters and phone calls relating the spiritual and metaphysical experiences of hundreds of people who received readings to healing sessions with me. These are some of those testimonies and accounts. I have witnessed miraculous healings, epiphanies and life changing happenings events. I have met people from every habitable continent on the Earth by making the decision to grow this amazing connection to Spirit, to share it with all the open minds and hearts out there. From Alabama to Australia, we understand each other! These are the people who opened the Light in their hearts enough to feel, hear and touch the Other Side in a myriad of ways. I am blessed to be a part of this incredible ascension process with so many awakened and beautiful Souls. They have related their experiences in their own words. I am ever grateful!

Some of the communication I've received over the years. They are listed in Random Order From 2007 to 2014:

Judi,

Thank You! You hit everything right on! And now that I think back, how could you ever have known my mothers name and my Grandmothers name?

Sending Hugs,

Liz F., Alabama

Dear Judi,

I just wanted you to know how grateful I was yesterday to meet you and receive such a compassionate and profound reading from you! you are a truly remarkable person!! Blessings to you!!!

Simong, Hawaii

Oh Judi...you have been on my mind so much since the other night. Everything that came through to me - the validations, the words and wisdom from the angels and our guides. I have felt Edward with me endlessly since that evening.... the healing energy that was being created WOW. Edward was there and held my hand the whole time...at least I believe the whole time as there were moments I was clearly not on the table. I have been told by Kerri, my friend, that at one point my legs were levitated off the table. What an incredible experience. Thank you to you for being an AMAZING part of this journey...being put into contact with Edward has been overwhelming to me.

I thank you, again, from the bottom of my heart...

Many blessings to you Love and Light xo

Charlotte, Canada

You are so good, Judi. I've just been singing your praises. I've had friends over the years who are psychic and love them, but you are especially gifted. You are wonderful. Hugs to you too! I'll keep you posted as to my progress. H.G. South Carolina

Hi Judi
I just wanted to thank you again for the session it was amazing!!!
Randy, New Jersey

Hi Judi! I loved your workshop! Learned SO much, and made such a strong connection in the
meditation....we were meant to meet!!
D.L. Louisiana

Hello! I started painting again! Normally, it takes me days or weeks to finish one but I have done 4 since I saw you! I also started doing the guided meditations you recommended and so far I feel wonderful.
Thank you again!
:-)
Veronica, Alabama

So the day before yesterday my sister told me that she wanted to move to Arizona and that her boyfriend loves sailing and wants to buy a sailboat one day. I can't believe you were able to pick up on that! I really appreciate how open and comfortable you made the experience for me and will be referring plenty of people to you in the future! I've been meditating and trying to communicate with my spirit guides, so if you have any advice for me, I'd love to hear it.

Thank you so much again! You set my heart at ease.
Katie, Alabama

Judi,

I just want to say thank you again for the healing that you put in my heart. I feel stronger now and know that it will continue to grow... believe me you will be hearing from me again...
Jenny

Judi, Thank you again for sharing your gift and your insight with me -- I've never had an experience like that before and I'm really glad I had the opportunity to meet you and talk with you. I've felt a little more at ease, definitely more optimistic, and I think also a lot more open to embracing my spiritual side than I have been in a long time. Thank you!
Stacy, Alabama

OMG Judi, your the best, I'm going to find a way to spread the news about you, actually I have a site myself, Can I add you on my site as like a recommended link, etc? You didn't know x&%$ about me and you and your guides nailed it. Love ya!!

Lori Z. Ohio

Dear Judi,

I wanted to thank you for sharing your gift with me! I had an inspiring afternoon with you and believe my life will be forever changed as a result! You provided me with the best Christmas present ever!

I wish you and yours a very Merry Christmas and a healthy and happy New Year!

Thank you & bless you,

Kim, Alabama

Judi -

They were right!

My Spirit Guides said that I would find an job doing something I had not done before, but using skills I already had. I start Monday where I worked three years ago. I will have full medical benefits! Salary instead of commission!

Thanks for all your support and encouragement.

Lee, Alabama

Hi Judi!

I just want to say thank you for the reading and the great conversation this afternoon! It was quite an amazing experience! After the healing session, I felt an intense sense of lightness of being. After a few hours, I'm still feeling that somewhat euphoric sensation. You are truly amazing in your abilities, and I appreciate all the information you gave me. Everything we talked about and everything you wrote down for me was so informative and quite accurate. I really enjoyed laughing so much with you. You made me feel quite comfortable. I'll definitely recommend you to anyone interested in a reading, and I hope to see you again in the future for perhaps another healing session (if this one ever wears off) or to get an update from my guides on the many perplexities that I may face in life.

Thanks so much!

Tim, Alabama

This Healing Light Energy is very powerful. Not only was my thigh healed but most of the inflammation problems in both hips has been removed. Hopefully the healing energy will spread as many are in need now. I am amazed at the good work you do- far beyond what most churches do. The entire community should be grateful."

Jim, Alabama

My neck is totally well! Feels the best it has felt in weeks. I feel like a new person. Thank You!!! Thank you and all our blessed guides!!!!!

Donna, Alabama

WOW...that was some session. You sure have tuned in to your guides to be able to communicate like you do. I was encouraged to get back to the White Light.

Thanks again,

Vicki, Alabama

I got out in the yard and worked this afternoon. I could not have done this before the healing that took place last Sunday March 1, 2009. The healing happened. I feel so very blessed! Thank you for your role in my healing. Most Sincerely,

Jean, Alabama

I'm sending up thanks to the universe in general but I did want to thank you for your part and to please don't stop what you're doing because we're feeling the love from here in Huntsville all the way to Vandy! Blessings to you!

Beth, Alabama

Judi,

I am immensely grateful for all that you have shared with us, and for the spiritual connections that you have helped establish. I found your meditations to be extremely powerful. You have opened so many doors, introduced so many new ideas and have actualized the experience well beyond words in a book. I think of your classes as a miraculous time. And I suspect it's true for all of us. Just want you to know that.

Janis, Alabama

Judi,

I am so grateful to God, my healers, and you, Judi for the healing that has taken place! The healing (session) felt like tissue was being forced through a narrow place back to where it belonged. Like pulling a loose balloon through the entrance of the neck of a bottle. Amazing! Yes, a miracle :)!!!

Much Love and Gratitude

Jean, Alabama

Judi,

I met you on Saturday, I came to your church...You told me my Spirit Guide's name and told me to ask to feel the energy. The most beautiful thing happened last night. I sat quietly to do my meditation. I spoke aloud and asked to let me feel this energy. My whole body instantly felt electrostatic charged. It was like a pulsating wave, the feeling was so intense and lasted about a minute or two. I could hardly sleep last night and awoke refreshed with new eyes to the world this morning. I wouldn't have known how to do that this early in my spiritual journey without help. God bless you for what you do for others,

Christie, Alabama

 Hi Judi,

I really feel as if I were in a "dream state" all the way home. Thank you for opening up my channels. Love and Light,

Ayla, Alabama

I felt the love of the Holy Spirit engulfing me with peace and wholeness. I feel that my burden has been lifted. Now the anxiety and depression is gone. May the blessings of the Holy Spirit come to you,

Jim, Alabama

Judi,

I was looking for clarification and boy was it clear!" I am still knocked over by the show of energy...thanks for understanding, verifying and just being you. Blessings!

Ernesta, Alabama

Hi,

I know that my guides did lead me to you, Judi. without your guidance, I did not know how to build the energy and so on. Right before I came this site...I did not know what to do with this...tingling and feeling vibration on my palms so...I was kind of giving up trying and since I met you and started learning this...tingling and vibration got stronger rapidly. I will not ignore this anymore I will build it stronger and take the purpose of this. After all this is what I have been wanting to do!

Again...judi.....YOU ROCK!!!

HUGS

Much Love and Respect,

Kumi, Idaho

"Thank you! I am feeling much better after our session this week. It really helped me to get through. I shared your messages with my brother-in-law and he was amazed. I will keep my sunglasses at hand".

Thanks again,

Ron D. Alabama

Judi-

The best thing that has happened to me in years is you channeling the energy to open my crown chakra! It has made all the difference in the world. My mind is clearer and thoughts don't get stuck in a loop like they used to. My sinuses still hurt off and on but I always think of how my crown chakra is open now and I bring a huge tube of Light in and I start buzzing and relax instantly. Thanks again so very much! Looking forward to seeing you again soon here in Madison.

Michella, Alabama

Cuddles and I at the Humane Society Parade in Mentone, Alabama 2013.

16
FRIENDS WITH LIGHTS,
A TRUE STORY
BY PSYCHIC MEDIUM & HEALING CHANNEL
JUDI LYNCH

In 2012 I released a 42 page book entitled Friends With Lights, A True Story. The book documents some of my early childhood, teenage and later experiences as an adult who decided to open up to the possibilities of the Soul and how we are blessed to be able to communicate with our loved ones in Heaven. I have learned so much since I started delivering messages and facilitating healing energy sessions in 2006! My education has mostly been working with the amazing Souls brought to my life because of this work. Some of the first messages I received from spirit were for my brand new next door neighbor Liz from her late Mother. Detailed and incredible, those messages filled my heart with a radiance I could never have imagined. Liz crossed over in January of 2014. I will always miss her being next door even though I know where she is. God Bless you Liz. Thank You for being a part of this journey.

This is Liz Fischer's review of Friends With Lights, A True Story published on Amazon by Liz on September 29, 2012.

I met Judi about 8 years ago when my husband Mike and I moved next door to her. I was not aware of her abilities until one day she just came over, we had not even met yet but there she was with some written messages for me from the other side.

I was astonished as I read these messages and I started to cry because how could she know these things? Names of my then deceased mothers co-workers. Sayings, like brush your hair, as my Grandmother always told me. I have experienced these things myself throughout my own life but to have a then stranger confirm my beliefs was so comforting to me. Startling but comforting none the less.

She has told me the name of my Guardian Angel and I could not believe it because the name has deep meaning for me.

Judi is truly gifted and this book is a gift from her to all of us. It is a thought provoking read.

CONSCIOUS ASCENSION

Friends with Lights

A True Story

by Judi Lynch

CONTENTS

Dedication

Prologue

Cover Photo, "Barn Orb" by Judi Lynch

Dedication

This book is dedicated to every soul who thought they were lost until they found a friend with a light. Also to my baby girlfriend Anni Lu, sweetest dog I ever knew. Rest in beautiful peace, sweet girl.

We are beings of Shining Light, Loved Unconditionally.

Prologue

My earliest memory of life on Earth began when I was four years old. It was my birthday party and I remember a huge, bright light setting me down at a picnic table in our backyard. In a matter of seconds, I was opening my presents. One of those presents was a little stuffed cat made with rabbit fur. It looked real! I said, "Whose bright idea was this! I'm not allowed to have a cat!" Everyone laughed. I have no memory of things before that and I told friends all through my childhood about that Light. I didn't know what it was or what it meant but I could never forget it. I was so bright yet it didn't hurt my eyes and I remember looking up and thinking I had just arrived from somewhere else. Where, I didn't know.

When I was five I had no idea what was going on in my world other's couldn't see. I told my Grandma Lucy her husband was sitting on the couch next to her one day. She said I sure was mean because I knew he had been dead for many years. I said I knew that he was, but he was still sitting right there! I told my mom that grandma sure needed some new glasses! We made friends later when she showed me how to play solitaire and blackjack, I told her I'd be quiet about it if I saw anyone else sitting there and playing cards with us that she couldn't see.

I also remember falling asleep during nap time once at school and seeing my friend Denise fall down, scraping her knee out on the playground during her class recess. I woke up wondering if she was okay. After school she showed me her injury. I didn't know then what Astral Travel was. I only knew I had wanted to be outside on the playground all the time so I guess I must have traveled there whenever I got the chance. These memories helped me in my journey later in life.

Chapter One

Visiting Souls

When I was nine, my friend's mother was killed in a train accident just a couple of blocks from our back door. I was sitting in my room when her mother came to me and told me to please tell everyone that she was okay, she was in Heaven. She wanted her kids to know she would always send help to watch over them. I ran down the street and told my friend that her mom wasn't dead. I said I had just seen and talked to her at our house! She was floating in the air in a big light! My friend ran down to our house to see and told my mom what I had said. My mother slapped me across the face and I cried all night long. My eyes were so swollen that I could hardly see the next day. I knew she had been there but no one believed me. I thought I was doing something good to help my friend. I was too young to understand why I had gotten in so much trouble. A short time later my little friend took a hammer and broke apart a huge amethyst crystal that belonged to her Dad, giving me a big piece. She said I should have it but she didn't know why. That crystal is now sitting on my dresser all these years later after always being in my jewelry box. I never forgot where it came from. It was special to me for many reasons, some I didn't know until later.

I spent the first few years of my childhood attending a Southern Baptist Church every week. They told us we were all sinners and if we didn't obey the words in the Bible, we were all going to Hell. I questioned everything. I was told to be quiet, listen and obey. The Summer I turned eleven, I went to Baptist camp in rural Indiana. One afternoon while I was out enjoying the day's activities, one of the camp counselors broke into my suitcase. She took a seam ripper and ripped the seams out of all my new dresses, saying they were too short. I never went back to the Baptist church again. I wasn't about to follow their silly rules. I had a faith that no one could shake and none of these people could answer my questions or explain how I knew things or saw things they couldn't see. When I was twelve, I joined a Methodist church because they had a youth group and we could wear whatever we wanted.

Though I had asked for the visiting souls to go away, I still had a few more encounters I explained away as dreams. One of those visits occurred in high school when I was 16. I woke up one morning knowing what had happened to my friend's boyfriend the night before. He had been in a horrible car accident on his way home from a family celebration, he came to me and told me how much he cared about her, to please make sure she knew. That morning I woke up and called her house immediately, she told me his sister had just called her to let her know. She asked me how I knew about it. Why would his sister call me? It was 7 in the morning. I was confused and didn't know exactly what to say. I told her that his sister must have called when I was half asleep. I knew everything that had happened in the accident and I told her I was coming over. In this crazy dream I thought I'd had, he had begged me to go and see if she was all right. She insisted that her mother was there and she would get through this. She said I really didn't have to come over. I still felt this overwhelming need to comfort her even though I didn't understand it. I went to her house later that morning and I knew without a doubt that the information I had received wasn't a dream. I know I woke up in the middle of the night and he was there, he told me about the accident and about his feelings for my friend. He was just a teenager, he had a whole life in front of him, and he was gone in an instant.

Later that year another friend died violently in a home invasion. He also visited me one night and told me that he had been getting up his nerve to finally ask me out on a date then suddenly he was in the wrong place at the wrong time. He told me it had seemed so unreal when it happened. Again, I thought his visit had just been a dream of wishful thinking, but a girl I knew told me the very same thing at his funeral. She walked up to me and said, "Did you know that he had a crush on you but was too shy to say anything?" Yes, I knew, but I didn't tell her how he had told me.

Not too long after that, I woke up in the middle of the night thinking that another friend's boyfriend had somehow gotten in my bedroom. He was standing at the end of my bed telling me he needed my help. I said you are not supposed to be in my room! How did you get in here? He said I think I'm in trouble and I need to know where to go. I told him to go home and he said that he tried, no one could see him there. He told me he had walked right through everyone! I said, "Oh No! That means you're supposed to go to heaven then." He told me that was all he needed to know and thanked me for my help. I went back to sleep probably thinking what wonderful, ridiculous dreams I have! The next afternoon someone called to tell me he had been killed in a motorcycle accident. I told them I already knew but I didn't know who had called me, I must have been asleep. Again, I didn't know what else to say.

My first real job at 16 was working in the basement of a cemetery as a telemarketer. We had to call people every evening after dinner, and ask them if they had a burial plot for the big day. A great job for a psychic teenager! I used to try and scare everyone by telling them there was a ghost on the stairs or something in the closet. We had some frightening times the night thunderstorms knocked the power out.

Chapter Two

Life Changing Events

I have lived my life gathering experiences, friends and knowledge. I always knew I had certain "psychic things" going on but it wasn't something I had time to focus on. I also had lots of knowledge and love for music and entertainment. As a child and young adult I took classes in dance, guitar, piano, music theory and performed in choirs for several years. As an adult I started writing and recording my own music. I performed with several bands and I had the amazing experience of recording in some of the best studios in Nashville plus working with many gifted and famous musicians and producers. I have to be completely honest and admit I was deeply disappointed by the treatment of women in the industry. I didn't stop writing but I was disillusioned. My dream of writing songs for established artists was left behind even though I had signed several song contracts, I stopped going to songwriters nights and I stopped recording. I bought a computer and taught myself how to do graphic design.

In the early 1990's, I had left Northwest Indiana for North Alabama. There was so much negative energy and rage. Near Chicago and the surrounding areas that I felt extremely anxious. Several people I knew had recently been murdered and the tone was dangerous. A friend's daughter and my lawyer were both murdered. One morning our neighbor was killed by a bomb wired to his truck ignition. There were problems with gangs and our neighborhood was rapidly changing. I grew very anxious and concerned. Even going out alone to the grocery store or the mall was a stressful ordeal. I felt such a strong pull to move away from there, to change our lives and live somewhere not quite so angry and violent. Everything there felt so gray to me. Yes, gray is the word for it. I couldn't see any light there anymore at all. A big part of me knew I had to get closer to the Earth and breathe in the air to heal from all the stress and trauma.

One very profound psychic experience happened in Indiana before my family and I moved. My husband and I were riding in the back of a friend's car on our way to play carpet golf with him and his wife. I had an acute anxiety attack while we were driving. I told my husband to never ever get in the car with this friend again! Even though I didn't know where or when, there was going to be a life changing accident. I had heard a loud boom and twisting metal, it haunted my thoughts everyday. We continued to go places and spend time with them but we always drove ourselves to the activities from then on. He warned his friend about my "premonition" but they laughed it off saying it was because he drove too fast and made me nervous. I knew it was more than that. A few months later this friend invited my husband to go to Chicago for a Bears game. Free tickets and the Bears! I knew he wanted to go but I begged him to please politely decline the tickets unless he was going to drive. He remembered my warning and politely declined the invite, saying we had other plans.

Early that Sunday morning, we received a phone call from our friend's wife. He had been killed on his way to pick up the Bears tickets from his parent's home. His car was hit and completely demolished by a fast moving train. The warning signals had not been installed yet and were lying in the grass by the tracks. If my husband had said yes to the trip, he would have been in that car. He lost one of his best friends that day and he told me he would never doubt my ability to "know" things again.

Chapter Three

Shining Lights

We needed a quieter life; we sold the house, quit our jobs, packed up everything and moved. I felt I was on my way to changing my life by slowing down, opening up heart and mind, and discovering a whole different way of thinking. I was turning down the noise. I also had a very real warning that my father's health was going to worsen. He had taken early retirement, he and most of the rest of my family were in Alabama now.

Two years after I moved, my paternal Grandmother died after complications from pneumonia and flu after a car accident. A few months later, my Father died from cancer. One morning I woke up and my Grandmother was standing in my room near the dresser. Then she faded out and was gone. I missed them both dearly. My house was between where both of them had lived.

It was because of my grief that I started reading about things I had never read about before. I found a book called *Adventures of a Psychic* about Sylvia Browne. This woman claimed she could get messages from those on the other side. I loved her personality, she made me laugh. She also gave me comfort and hope. I also agreed with the spiritual information she was sharing and it made so much sense to the way I also believed things to be.

One morning I woke up, jumped out of bed and ran to the window. I saw a huge silent light shining down on the lawn. So bright, but it didn't hurt my eyes! So calming, so warm, it felt like a big hug of love. The light I had seen as a child was back and it looked like it was parked over my house. It looked like a helicopter was hovering over, shining a spotlight down on me. I might have thought it was a helicopter if it hadn't been completely silent. This was a sign to me I was finding that Light I had long ago forgotten was available to me. I was wide awake and I know what I saw.

One day a friend at work handed me a book and said it changed her life. I could hardly put it down. Why did all of this sound so familiar? Could all of this really be possible? Why does it make so much sense to me? The book was the *Celestine Prophecy* by James Redfield. So thank you Linda C. Owen wherever you are now! When I met you, you were a graphic designer who wanted to study energy healing. You gave me this book and you moved to Utah, I never saw you again. You are one of the people who helped me to change my life and find a deeper purpose.

I finished that book and thought about all these new concepts I wanted to explore. I went to the used book store just down the highway and I looked for anything they might have about psychic communication. I wanted to know more about how I could communicate again. The only book they had on the shelf about this was *We Don't Die, George Anderson's Conversations with the Other Side* by Joel Martin and Patricia Romanowski. On the back of the book it said, "This is a book that will open your mind to an infinite realm of possibility, reassurance, and spiritual growth." It was so true!

I was truly fascinated with the people who were communicating. I wanted to understand and know more. I read more books by these authors and several others to keep these concepts flowing in my mind. I didn't know too many people personally that I could discuss this with. These books also truly made me understand I had to get myself back on track and find my spiritual self. For the next several years, I worked on trying to be the person I needed to be inside. I read, I experienced, I wrote, I went out and lived a life. I sought out new adventures and made new friends. I worked on myself because I knew I had let myself get gray and careless. I had felt so overwhelmed with all the things I could not control around me. I started applying the concepts I learned to my life and everything started to change for the better. I knew I had life themes to complete or overcome and I learned better how to deal with other people who didn't understand me. I worked on keeping my energy positive and removing myself from as much negativity as possible.

During 2005 I went through a lot of changes in my life. I had quit my graphic design job working on a NASA contract for a big company contractor. For several reasons (the major one being the constant neck pain and migraines), I decided I wanted to have a career where I could work at home. So I studied interior decorating and design with a couple of online and correspondence courses and started a small business. My pain was still there but at least I could make my own hours plus set my own goals.

I also started spending more time on my spiritual studies and writing down goals. I joined an online community to gain more knowledge. I reread books that rang true to my psychic soul. I had time to think about my life and I also knew that my neck pain was getting worse, my migraines were more severe. Throughout the years, I had been to several doctors about the curvature in my neck, the disc problems and bone spurs, etc. The last doctor (a neurologist) told me I could never live with this pain, and I would have to have surgery sooner or later. I opted for never. The problems were too close to my spine and I knew there was no guarantee I would ever be out of pain or if what they wanted to do would require a lifetime of more surgeries or procedures. I knew there was something else out there coming along to help me but I didn't know what it was yet. During this time I adopted a little Jack Russell terrier mix named Anni, and her sweet personality helped me when I was in a lot of pain. She channels great energy and unconditional love.

I pressed on with my little business but I spent a lot of time hurting and recovering. I got very depressed but it was just what I needed to wake up. Listen to what my body was telling me. It was time to heal. Time to heal everything! I was ready. I kept praying, listening, meditating, reading and discovering. I asked for my spiritual gifts to be made stronger and the Universe set up a chain reaction of events to make it happen. It might be a cliché', but you really better be ready for what you ask for!

Chapter Four

Awakening the Energy

At the suggestion of several people in an online spiritual discussion group, I made plans to attend the Galactic Expo in Nashville in the Spring of 2006. I had no idea I was going to feel the rush of Soul energies and float away on a cloud that day, but I did.

The discussion group had suggested a couple of people for me to stop by and talk to or have a reading with. I sought out those people. The first one was a psychic named Sean who told me several interesting things about myself along with this "You have many gifts, and more are coming to you which you will learn how to use." He was very intuitive and informative, he gave me a marvelous confidence I was supposed to be there that day.

One of my most important objectives at the New Age Expo was finding Dr. Mallory Elliott. I was told I should really try to meet and talk with her or attend her seminar there at the expo. I walked up to her booth and I told her my friends had recommended I see her while I was there. She didn't ask my name and she asked me to sit down in one of two chairs. I sat down and she stood behind me. I could feel the heat and the energy even though I could not see her, she never physically touched me. I felt energy above my head and behind me. I closed my eyes and she started the meditation. She told me she was taking me on a light journey to the other side. Pretty soon it felt as if we were floating and I could feel white light pouring in through the top of my head. I felt so light and so free, it was the feeling of peace and happiness I had remembered feeling what seemed like an eternity ago. All the negativity was melting away. It was awesome and glorious, taking away all my fears and doubts about anything. Angels, lots of them, standing in that same Light I had seen before. So bright, but soft at the same time, you can look right into it. There are no more words I can think to write to describe it.

When we came back to the reality of the booth in the middle of the expo building, she picked up the other chair and moved it closer to mine, sitting right next to me. She almost whispered in my ear, "There is no other way to put this to you, because we don't believe in hiding the truth, and you have found your way to me now. You are incredibly gifted psychically with more to come if you want and ask for it to. You are someone who already has the power to ask for anything you want, just ask. Surround yourself with light consciousness. The connection is already there. I'm sure you already know this."

I was still stuck to the chair in awe. I know what I saw, I know what I felt. It validated all these wild and crazy things that had been happening all my life. All the warnings, visits from spirits, white lights and synchronicity, made more sense now. Everything that has happened to me that led me to this place right here today. There were two people waiting in line to speak with her, so I told her I would be back later in the afternoon with a question or two. I walked back to her booth a couple of hours later and asked for her advice. Should I take classes? What could I do with these "gifts?" She told me her visions. She said "You certainly don't need my help to communicate with Spirit; you do it all the time. You are going to find you own way to communicate with Spirit and use these gifts, you can pretty much ask for anything, it's up to you to decide." She asked me if I thought it was my purpose to be a healer. She asked me how I wanted to be able to talk to Spirit, that I could decide and all I really needed was confidence it could be done. I asked her if she could explain to me how I could communicate directly (see, hear out loud) and she said I had my own way of doing things, it would become more clear to me. I thanked her with all my heart and floated off into the afternoon.

I may have forgotten how to see them but I could feel them everywhere at that expo, all around me. There were souls gathered there from all over, they were even making the curtains swish back and forth. It was the happiest I had felt in a long time and physically I was in relief. It was absolutely awesome! My pain was diminished and leaving me and I felt like I was actually walking on air.

April, 2006 Dr. Mallory-Elliott (on the left),

and me (on the right).

<u>**Chapter Five**</u>

The Crystal and the Spirit Guide

When I returned home in Alabama I was frantic to find a clear crystal pendulum someone had given me a couple of years before. I used to have it hanging in a window and I had never gotten around to putting it up again. I found it in a drawer. I wanted to feel that energy coming through. I had to know if I could really start communicating the way I wanted to so badly. I had so many friends and loved ones I missed. Could they find me? I knew from all my studies and experiences that we were all supposed to have a Spirit Guide around us. I wanted this guide to validate their presence and their identity. I kept asking questions, holding the pendulum steady between my fingers, watching the energy give me the answers. Back and forth for yes, round in a circle for no. The pattern never changed, it always gave me that formula and all the answers were strong and made sense.

I also started listening to the Ascension Meditation CD by Dr. Louise Mallory-Elliott every single night before bed. Dr. Mallory-Elliott is the same woman who gave me the five minute session back at the Galactic Expo, and opened up what I now know is my Crown Chakra. She helped me to let the Light back in. Thank God for wonderful Souls like Louise! An online spiritual friend named Char had sent me the CD months before, but it wasn't until I met Louise in person did I realized how special these meditations were!

I worked on this day and night, the energy grew stronger and stronger. Pretty soon I needed to be able to grow beyond yes and no using the crystal. I needed to know who was out there. I needed more validation. It was at the point I knew I had messages coming through that I could not hear and I had to know what they were. I didn't want to just "know" things anymore. I had to feel it and see it again. I asked for it and prayed for it to be.

With extreme determination I got a piece of paper and wrote the alphabet one morning. I took the pendulum and I moved it over the letters to see if the energy would pull to spell out anything. I wanted anything that would tell me something in more detail. I knew my guide was helping but I wanted a name. I wanted information and more communication. I was not going to let this go. I could physically feel the energy growing around me. I also learned very quickly you had better remember to say your prayers, and light those white candles, because a couple of ghosts almost scared me half to death. Although they couldn't harm me, I wasn't ready for the answers to the questions that I asked one of them.

The first time I held that crystal pendulum over that letter chart, I could not comprehend what was happening. The dowser started pulling from letter to letter spelling out words. I sat there staring down at the table for what seemed like several minutes, wondering if I had imagined it. Was I just really tired or was I now getting letters and words? This energy was talking to me. Though who was I talking to?

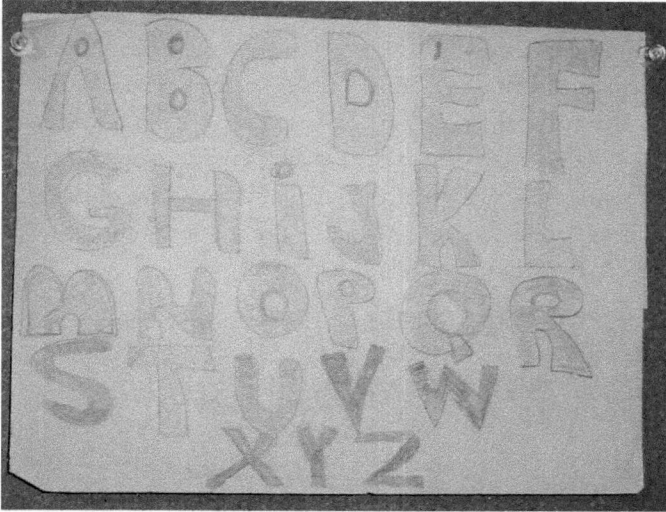

Judi's handwritten letter chart

I started asking questions and I started getting answers. The first word spelled out to me was "Jack." I asked if he was my Spirit Guide. The answer was yes. I asked who else was there. The answer was "Emma." Emma's energy was very different somehow and I asked her who she was. Her answer on the letter chart was "ghost." I jumped up from the table! I had not expected that! I put everything away and I went to bed.

The next morning (after tossing and turning all night) I tried again. This time I lit a candle, I said a prayer, and I asked Jack not to bring anymore ghosts around. I wasn't ready for it. I asked to communicate with him and he started talking. It took hours and hours to work this way. He was channeling words and sentences through the crystal in my right hand over a letter chart while I wrote them down with my left hand. He answered questions and gave me advice. One of the first things he told me was to read Dyer. I thought he must be talking about Wayne Dyer and when I asked, the answer was yes. Jack told me about the life he had lived on Earth before agreeing to become my spirit guide and a whole lot more.

I got brave enough one day, asking about several of my friends and loved ones. I inquired about an old caving and hiking buddy (and good friend) of mine who had crossed over in 2001, the next thing I knew, he was there. We channeled several messages and then…

I asked him about another friend who had been in a car accident the year before. Had he seen him there on the Other Side? His answer was no. I asked Jack if my friend was there in Heaven. His answer was no. I knew something was wrong. If he wasn't there, where else would he be? Were they not getting through correctly? What was it I didn't understand? There was no doubting this incredible energy and all the other communication I was getting. I guess I had to find him then. I had to know.

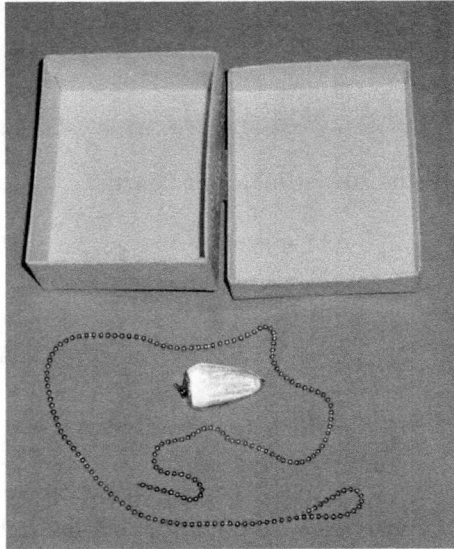

Judi's first crystal pendulum

Chapter Six
Where are you?

Determined to find out what was going on, I sat down the next morning and asked my friend if he was here, was he around me? The energy running through my pendulum answered yes. I asked him if he was all right and he answered no. My first instinct was to think he was still just a little mad about why he had died so young and he wanted to express it. The more the messages came through, it became clear he was not where he was supposed to be. Why I didn't understand?

If I could communicate with him and he wasn't on the Other Side, then that could only have meant he had stayed here. If he had stayed here, then how did he find me? How was he communicating with me if he was a ghost? I had asked for a hold on that, please!

He was in a complete spiritual panic, but at the same time we could not believe we were talking to each other. Of course, the reason we could communicate is because I spoke to him, his energy came through and he had been looking for someone to help him. He really heard me say his name! "Mike, are you there?"

I stayed confused for awhile but I kept asking questions. Then I realized he was afraid to cross over. I could not believe this had really happened to him. He said he did not understand what was in that Light and he wasn't going. He asked me what would happen to him when he got there. He wanted to know what kind of trouble he was in and he was afraid they wouldn't even let him in. I asked him what was happening to him now where he was. I was sorry I asked!

He said where he was he was being chased by mean spirits and he said he had not lived his life like he should have. He was afraid of being judged. He said he had checked on his family and friends after the accident and they had suspected him of drinking and driving that evening (which he had not done). He said he had become so upset by this he had stayed around to try to make them hear or see him somehow, but he soon realized they couldn't. No one could hear him, no one could see him. Until I picked up that crystal and he heard me say his name through the consciousness.

Chapter Seven

A Friend with a Light

Once I realized what was going on I asked him if he could see a Light where he was. He said yes, a little bit, that he could see a little bit of a bright light. Then he asked me if I could see him sitting on a box in front of the table I was sitting at. I said no. I know you're here, your words are getting through, but I cannot see you with my eyes. His words were being channeled through the crystal the same way my guides were, though his energy was frantic and panicked. He kept asking me if I could see him and his energy kept moving around the room. He wouldn't cross over and he didn't want me to stop channeling. He asked me to call a friend of ours, Lucy, with some information she would understand. To tell her something I would never have known. He wanted me to tell her he had seen her, and her family, do something very special for him. I called her and told her Mike was communicating with me and what was he told me. She said the three of them had stood in a prayer circle for Mike. Validation! It took me five whole days to convince him to step closer to that Light. I asked my guide for help and I asked my friend JV (who had already come through) for help.

They described to me in every detail what happened when Mike crossed into that Light and I wrote down every single word. It took hours for them to spell out the celebration that took place on the Other Side, the messages that started coming through were breathtaking and wonderful. That was only the beginning of the messages and the miracles to come. The biggest miracle was I had found someone I did not know was lost. I found someone I did not understand that I had the ability to find. It was the most amazing thing I could have ever been a part of. I could translate every word. It was incredible!

I had pushed these things out of my mind for so long, now not only did I have to accept this direct communication but I had just helped a Soul cross over. The energy increased by trifold!. So did the messages, so did the visits, and then the healings started.

I had gone to the Galactic Expo to get a psychic reading and have a little fun! Imagine, I was channeling information with my right hand and a crystal plus writing it all down with my left!

These are his pleas...

Messages started coming in, stronger and stronger, hundreds and hundreds of words to write down. Mike started telling me how he was literally trapped on this soul plane, what he saw and experienced, and why. My utter amazement that this was happening was also comforted by the fact I emailed Dr. Mallory-Elliott to make sure this really was happening! She explained to me if he had died suddenly in a violent crash and he had rejected going into the Light, it was not an uncommon occurrence for a soul to become lost this way.

His channeled words:

"I heard Judi channeling and communicating. She was using a pendulum and a piece of paper with the alphabet written on it. She got my message. She spelled out my name. I couldn't believe we were able to communicate this way. I told Judi that I thought my soul was damned to hell. I had witnessed someone close to me performing a ceremony from a book. They were mad because I had left too soon and they wanted revenge. Judi told me this wasn't true and that no one had the power to do such a thing to me. I didn't believe her at first.

She became very insistent that I go to the light. She asked me if I could see it and I said yes, a little bit, far off. She called to our friend JV and asked him to come and help along with her Spirit Guide, Jack. The next thing I knew I could see JV standing there. I said "Look, a friend with a light!" I shook his hand and he started laughing. "What took you so long to get here?" He could not understand why I had been hanging out with ghosts for all this time; he didn't comprehend why in the world I had not come to the light sooner. I explained to him what had traumatized me and he told me the same thing. No one has that kind of power over me. JV told me that Judi had done an awesome thing by saving me. He said that she was able to communicate with us.

JV said that he'd been trying for years before he crossed over to communicate with the other side without success. He said he heard Judi asking God to help me. He asked that her gifts be made stronger. God blessed Judi and said that her gifts would grow.

Her prayers had been heard and JV was asked to meet me at the light. JV said he was an Ascended Master and that Judi had accomplished something wonderful. She had helped save a soul."

This, about me? I felt like it had all happened in a blur, in another world way removed from this one, in a timeless existence where everything was wrapped in complete unconditional love and light. I always knew it was there but this was beyond anything I could ever have visualized or imagined to happen.

Here are excerpts from my emails to Dr. Mallory-Elliott:

From: Judi Lynch

Sent: Tuesday, May 02, 2006 3:12 PM
To: Dr. Mallory-Elliott
Subject: Seeking advice

Dear Dr. Mallory-Elliott,

I had the wonderful pleasure of having a short session with you at your booth recently in Nashville (at the New Age Expo). My name is Judi Lynch and my friends Char and Kim had suggested that I try to meet you that day.

My life has changed in a most awesome way since that Saturday when you sat down after our session and told me that I was extremely gifted. I knew about certain abilities I'd always had but I never imagined that they would grow into something like this. I began to meditate every day after that session and since then I have not only connected with my spirit guide but friends and family on the other side as well. I have had an incredible experience about a friend who had not yet crossed over after an accident last year and I need your advice. I want to be able to do automatic writing. It's of the utmost importance that I am able to record what he is telling me about his journey. Can you give me any advice on how to accomplish this?

Thank you so much. I hope to hear from you soon.

Judi Lynch

Her Reply:

Hi, Judi! I remember you well, and I am so glad for your effort at meditation and the many benefits it has brought to you. If the man is telling you about his journey, you can record it as he communicates it to you and transcribe it? I am confused by the phrase "automatic writing," which means dictation from another party in spirit, which still has to be written down. If you are hearing it now, why cannot you write it down? What am I missing here? Please let me know. Endless love, Louise

From: Judi Lynch [mailto:jalynch77@hotmail.com]
Sent: Wednesday, May 03, 2006 7:17 AM
To: Dr. Louise Mallory-Elliott

Subject: RE: Seeking advice

Hi Louise,

It's so nice to hear from you. Yes, I have left out a few facts :-). I'm not hearing him (yet), he is communicating with me through a crystal. He is spelling out all of his messages to me with a piece of paper that I wrote letters on. I can feel him standing next to me, I can feel his energy. He has moved objects and candle flames. I have passed along messages to people for him (that was so wonderful). He wants me to write down his story but at this rate, it could take a really, really long time! When I asked my SG for advice I was told to contact you. Could the answer be that I need to pray and meditate and ask to be able to hear him? Thank you so much for your help!

Much love to you,

Judi

Her Reply:

Honey bunny, if you can feel his standing there, and he can move objects by capitalizing on your energy field, there is no difference in hearing him or seeing him. Just start talking to him, and ASSUME that he is listening, and KNOW that you will be able to receive his responses. Start with something very simple like questions that can be answered yes or no. "Are you present? Do you wish to communicate? Are you in pain? Are you happy?" Then just wait to see what happens, realizing that sometimes, the answer comes when you are not concentrating and trying. Or, just start writing and see if you can feel where your style changes from that of your own. But this man is not yet dead? Is he is a coma? Endless love, Louise

From: Judi Lynch [mailto:jalynch77@hotmail.com]
Sent: Wednesday, May 03, 2006 10:12 AM
To: Dr. Louise Mallory-Elliott
Subject: RE: Seeking advice

Louise,

He was killed in a jeep accident in November of 2004. Of course I assumed that he had crossed over already. He came through to me one day while I was asking my SG questions - quite unexpected! He was so happy to know that he was getting through to me, he had been trying to communicate but said no one he had tried to talk to could hear him or feel him until now. He was in complete distress and afraid of where he was and where he was going. He kept telling me he was sorry for things that had happened, and that he was afraid of how he was leaving this world. This all happened over a period of several days. He asked me to give a message to three specific people (which I didn't understand why these three) I called these people and quickly understood why...these three had stood in a prayer circle for him recently and they understood. He went through a lot of emotional pain while he was here but he was a very loved and popular person. He was also very sensitive and judged himself too harshly. I think this is why he was having such a hard time, why he was so scared. And his passing was very, very traumatic.

During one session, I asked him if he could see a light, he said just a little bit. I asked him what else he could see and he said ghosts. I told him all about the light and what was there, I told him everything I knew and believed. I told him God loved him and he didn't belong where he was and he had to go. That people were waiting for him on the other side. He finally told me he was going to the light. I asked my SG to help him, to call on whoever had to be called to help him cross over. I then received the message from my SG that he had gone to the Light along with a "thank you" and "you are awesome Judi!" He has asked me now to write about his journey and I promised that I would. He says it is one of the things he has to do now. I hope this explains a little more of the situation :-) I have pages of his messages and he is still as silly as ever too!

Thank you Louise for your wonderful advice...I will let you know how things progress

In Love and Light

Judi

Her Reply:

OH! Now I understand! His soul went on to its own plane, but this portion of his personality was struggling. You did the right thing by helping him release himself into the light. Of course, he is still able to communicate from the other side. You already have more than enough to write down! So the only remaining problem is for you to open up not to needing the interface of alphabet letters. Just do it! Orient your mind to his and start writing down whatever comes to you; you will refine the process over time. Or type it at the computer, or record it. You are already receiving; you don't need letters anymore! Endless love, Louise

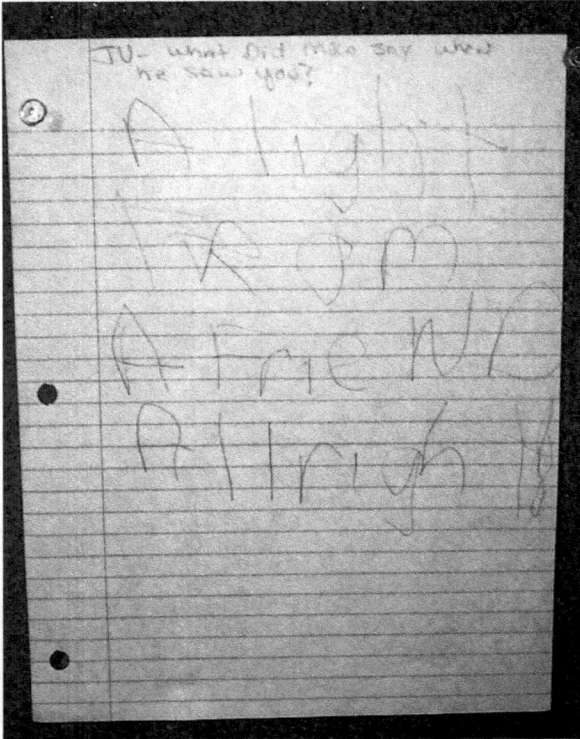

Channeled Message from Mike

Chapter Eight

Message for my Neighbor

On the morning of May 6, 2006 I received an important message from a Soul that would leave no doubt I was able to channel messages for other people I had never met or knew much of anything about. Her energy was very strong and insistent these messages get to the person they were intended for. The Soul had just crossed over.

Jack gave me several names and I wrote them down. These names were the Souls who were there to greet this person when they crossed over. Two of those souls had messages to go with the names. I wrote those down as well.

I was told these messages were for my new neighbor Liz who I had spoken to three times and not for more than ten minutes at one time. The last time was when she called and asked if we would keep an eye on their place because her mother had passed, they had to go out of town to her funeral. All I really knew about Liz and her husband was that they had moved here from Florida, he had family in this area, and they were fellow animal lovers.

I took out a piece of my stationary, I wrote down the date and all the names and the messages neatly, and put them in an envelope with her name on it. When I dotted the I in her name, I made a big circle. Not something I usually do.

I gathered up every bit of courage I didn't know I had and I called her on the phone. I told her I had something to tell her, and something to give her. I asked her to meet me out on the front porch. On my way over, I cut a white rose from one of our bushes and I met her on her front porch steps. I told her to have her husband come outside so we could have a witness and she called to him to join us. I told her I could communicate with the Souls on the Other Side and I needed her to see what I had written down for her, also that she might want to sit down.

She said "I'm okay, I don't have to sit, and I'd like to read it please." I took a deep breath and handed her the rose and the envelope. She opened up the envelope, started reading my note and I knew right away it was true. The tears welled up in her eyes, her hand went up to her mouth and she read it again and again and again. Then she grabbed me and hugged me so hard I thought she might break a rib. Validation!

When she had let go I said, "So, you know who these people are then?" She said, "Oh Yeah, Oh my God, Yes!" She finally sat down on the concrete and handed the note to her husband saying "You won't believe this, you just won't believe it. It's from my mother." He took the note out of her hand, read it, looked at me and said, "How did you do that?" I said I wasn't entirely sure yet how it all works but I knew that I was doing it. The messages and the names had all made sense and she also told me that when she was a girl, she always signed her name with a circle above the I.

I walked back home and sat down in silence for about an hour. That really did just happen. I just channeled accurate and detailed messages for my neighbor from her guides and loved ones. It took awhile for me to let it melt into my consciousness.

She walked over a few days later and told me that she kept the note next to her bed in the nightstand, how much it had helped her. Then she handed me a beautiful amethyst pendant as a thank you. It was still hard for me to believe the detail of the messages.

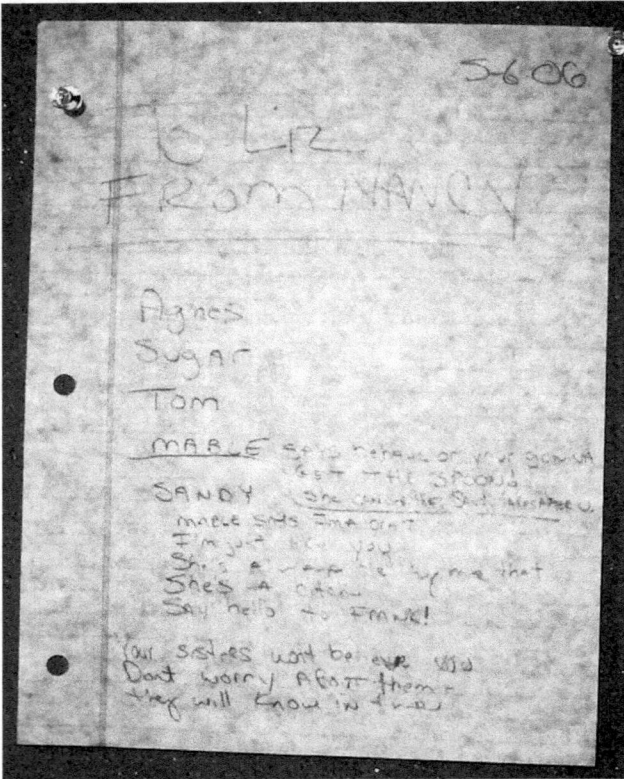

Channeled message for neighbor Liz Fischer

Chapter Nine

The First Healing

After I composed myself from delivering messages to my neighbor, I sat down at the table to communicate again.

It was explained to me that the damage in my neck was going to be healed through energy channeling. I had to sit very still and completely focus to watch in the crystal what was taking place. They were able to put on quite a spectacular show.

I sat motionless and focused my eyes on the huge chandelier crystal hanging on a large candle holder. I could see JV standing behind my reflection in the crystal, and actually see the healing taking place. There was a glow around my neck where the energy was being sent. I could feel the heat and the energy working inside my body at the same time. I was being healed by the most miraculous way anyone could ever imagine and I could actually see it taking place. I have no words to even describe what that was like or how I could ever explain it to someone else. My friends, guides and healers from the Other Side had found me and I was their first healing miracle.

In the next few weeks I received many other healings. My back, my sinus and my migraine headaches all received healing. My guides were able to channel energy to hold down my hands and feet so I could stay still during these procedures. Most of the time I could see what they were doing in the crystal. When the session was done, the heat and energy left my hands and I knew I could move again.

During this time, I played music and stayed up during all hours. Candle flames were dancing, light bulbs flickering and projected images were glowing in the crystal. Wonderful, beautiful, awesome images that would take your breath away when they came into focus. It was remarkable that my guides were channeling images into a chandelier crystal. I also got a lesson in how this energy feels when Souls try to pick up your foot or hold your hand. There was an actual pulse like a beating heart, it started in my hand and went all through my body. My hands levitated off the table and my feet lifted off the floor. It was incredible light and energy, a feeling of joy, complete unconditional love and healing.

One day, they projected Mother Theresa into the crystal, I sat and cried and cried. After that there was a gorgeous church and many visits from several different souls. I was listening to Coldplay, R.E.M., Alana Davis, John Mayer, Paul Simon and meditating, channeling and writing.

Chapter Ten

Soul Messages and Visits

Let the party begin! I started receiving messages, visits and information from everywhere.

My friend Mike who had just crossed over was very insistent I deliver several messages to the friends he had left behind here. Since he was also a friend of mine, I agreed to do that. I knew I had to brace myself for every reaction and try to be ready. It was incredible to me the amount of information he gave and it's accuracy. I was not only relaying the information, I was getting validation from several people that it was correct.

Over the next several weeks, I received message after message, visit after visit, and I wrote them all down in notebooks plus scraps of paper. Souls I had known in my childhood, people I used to know who had passed on, friends and relatives, guides and healers. The energy projected into the crystal was showing me things I could hardly believe. I was actually feeling their presence, their touch, and the healing energy they were channeling.

I started doing energy healings on my family and friends, we documented session after session. I would put my hands on their shoulders, build up the energy field, step back and let the guide energy take over to direct the healing where it was needed most. Amazing! We held meditation sessions with crystals and candles, asked for healing, getting messages and protection each time. I had never before even imagined in this life that it was possible to feel and hear and see so many miracles.

I have saved every letter, email, card and even phone message testimony to remind me that yes, it really is possible for all these things to happen, to keep happening in the future. I wanted everyone to know they had the ability inside of them to heal anything and the proof was out there. You can really touch another soul with this beautiful light to re-ignite the energy they possess inside, and awaken the gifts they have been waiting to remember how to use!

"Judi had become very confident in her psychic energy. I closed my eyes and concentrated on welling up my soul, as I call it. Feeling a glow and energy floating up from my feet and concentrating on the top of the well, a point above my head where the lights flow to. Judi put her hands on my shoulders." "Since then I have not had an asthma attack." Scott L.

"Thank you for the healing energy! My bumps and bruises are healing remarkably fast! In only 5 days it is like nothing happened to me at all. Some of my injuries were pretty bad and should not be healing as fast as they are, so thank you!" Liz F.

In March of 2007 I had my first healing energy workshop. The energy in the room that day was full of light with healing and smiling faces. It was the beginning of many readings, healings and friendships. More shining miracles for us all. It was awesome to feel so much support and understanding. We videotaped the whole workshop and I stayed for a couple of extra hours giving readings and healing sessions.

Healing Energy Miracles

Lecture and Workshop
with Healer and
Medium

Judi Lynch

Saturday, March 10th, 2007
1 p.m. to 4.p.m
Unity Church on the Mountain
Please call 256-536-2271 for reservations
LOVE OFFERING

Healer and Psychic Medium Judi Lynch will present a lecture and workshop on how her abilities to communicate with the souls on the Other Side were re-discovered. With this discovery, she found her purpose and spent months learning to channel the healing energy that healed her. God's Healing Energy can change your life . Judi is a self-taught energy channel and psychic medium with telepathic and audio abilities. Her abilities allow her to channel detailed messages from loved ones, give important information on your health and healing energy sessions for several different ailments.

The workshop will include testimonies from people who have already received messages, and healing energy sessions along with medical documentation. There will also be a demonstration of a healing session and a reading or two for the audience. Judi can also take requests for future sessions after the workshop and answer questions.

First advertisement for an energy healing workshop

76

Some of the testimonies I received after the Unity Workshop:

"The workshop Saturday was incredible. My friend and I attended and really came away energized. Judi, for this to have been your first was amazing! You were so relaxed and we both saw your beautiful white aura shining so brightly, and at times there were beautiful violet streams shooting out from you. Thank you so much for the wonderful workshop. We look forward to another." Carolanne

"I just want to say congratulations on a successful first workshop. I attended your work shop today at Unity and I must say it was awesome! I had some second guessing about attending after my mix-up with the time and being concerned about getting there late. But, I am so happy my guides continued to nudge me and I had to return for the workshop. I want to wish you much success as you move forward in your life purpose. I look forward to seeing your success and working with you on helping me discover my purpose as well. Thank you for sharing your experiences. Peace and many Blessings." Ernesta

"You were very on target with me and my friends at Unity today. It was a fun time too." Vicki

"I would like you to know it was a pleasure to meet you this past Saturday. You have an extremely wonderful gift and are using it to help others, and we commend you for all of your efforts." Brenda

"I went home so glad and feeling so light after that meeting that I wanted to share with you." "I am so glad to have met you and all those people! I have a feeling that after now my life will change forever." Adriana

"You have such a special gift. I know that these gifts are true and strong and you receive them because of your pure spirit and the desires of your heart. It is a privilege to have been at the workshop..." Dixie

After the workshop, I had weekly appointments for sessions. Every healing session and reading was one more miracle of light energy. I received notes, letters, emails and phone calls. It made me so happy to know that they could feel and experience this with me. I wanted everyone to know that this was the future of our evolution on Earth. This kind of healing and communication was out there for all of us. We have the capability to heal from so many things we carry around with us, along with healing our Souls, which need to be reminded of true capabilities and purposes here. I knew all of this was just the beginning of my journey in this part of my life. It was all new to me as a way of life here, but yet it wasn't. It was so familiar to every part of me.

Testimonies from sessions scheduled after the workshop:

"Thank you! I am feeling much better after our session this week. It really helped me to get through. I shared your messages with my brother-in-law and he was amazed. I will keep my sunglasses at hand! Thanks again," Ron D.

"The best thing that has happened to me in years is you channeling the energy to open my crown chakra! It has made all the difference in the world. My mind is clearer and thoughts don't get stuck in a loop like they used to. My sinuses still hurt off and on but I always think of how my crown chakra is open now and I bring a huge tube of Light in and I start buzzing and relax instantly.
Thanks again so very much!" Michella

"I am so glad I talked to you. I was looking for clarification and boy was it clear! I am still knocked over by the show of energy. I keep touching my hand just in awe. You are awesome- thanks for understanding, verifying and just being you." Ernesta

"Hello, gee, I didn't realize how much we were in another dimension or light energy until I pulled into Mac's. I feel surreal. Thank you, it was a wonderful session. Here's to white light," Vicki

Chapter Eleven

Sharing the Light

In the fall of 2007, we bought an old country church in Alabama up on Keel Mountain. It turned into the Crystal Healing & Spiritual Center along with a non-profit entity, The Crystal Healing Foundation, Inc..

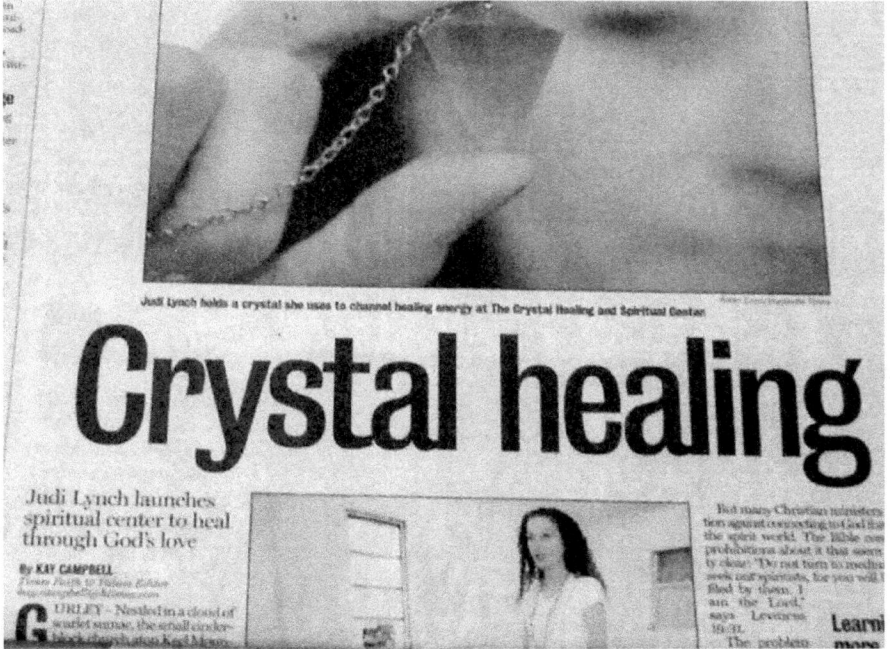

Judi Lynch holds a crystal she uses to channel healing energy at The Crystal Healing and Spiritual Center

Crystal healing

Judi Lynch launches spiritual center to heal through God's love

By KAY CAMPBELL
Times Faith to Faith Editor

GURLEY - Nestled in a cloud of scarlet sumac, the small cinder-block church on Keel Moun...

But many Christian ministers tion against connecting to God in the spirit world. The Bible con prohibitions about it this sternly clear: "Do not turn to mediu seek out spirits, for you will be filed by them. I am the Lord," says Leviticus 19:31.
The problem

Learn more

Huntsville Times, Fall 2008

I gave readings and healing sessions, taught classes and hosted workshops on psychic awareness, did energy healing and ascension for two years there until circumstances changed. I had to move. One afternoon after a reading, the crystal I was using to communicate fell out of my hand and I started hearing Souls without it. The energy being channeled through my hand was giving me the letters, words and messages. The person I had just given a reading to was an ordained minister and he had no idea the amazing energy field around him. He had come to ask me several questions about metaphysical and spiritual concepts and to tell me that people were seeing Angels at his church. I think an Angel must have been holding on to my hand when he left. I didn't need the crystal anymore. Amazing.

The journey continues since that day in the Spring when I discovered something amazing about the power of the light energy that communicates and heals us as we evolve our consciousness. There is a light that shines on us, for sure, always was and always will be. May you always know you have a Friend with a Light.

Endless Blessings, Peace and Healing Light Energy,

Judi

17

LIVING IN THE RAY OF LOVE AND WISDOM

In the design of the Universe, seven is quite a significant number. There are seven tones on the music scale, seven colors in a rainbow and seven streams of consciousness for a soul to become aware in. As we raise our frequency in attunement with these energy streams, we begin to understand how our roles here on Earth match the ray of our personality in this lifetime.

In spiritual terms, we incarnated here on Earth to evolve our souls through experiencing the light of the Source. This evolution seeks to end the divide between personality conflicts, to find atonement by shining a light on our best qualities. The inherent qualities from each of the seven rays of light consciousness combine to resonate a tone. This creates vibrant, amazing energy which meters our ultimate healing and ascension.

The second ray of awareness, or the blue ray, is described as the ray of love and wisdom. People becoming aware on this ray could be called the transformers. The energy they are able to feel, absorb and radiate is incredible. The life themes they face can be very challenging. They feel things on a higher level than others and they seek truth and love above all else. Their usual demeanor is patient and calm with a quiet strength plus a clear mind.

Their compassion is deep along with their need to love. That need, which lives in the truth seeker, produces wisdom on a higher level. When fully realized this wisdom breaks down barriers of judgment, hatred and religion to help others seek new enlightenment. They are the beautiful souls who facilitate animal rescue centers and recreation programs for the elderly. They could work in many different teaching, healing and creative professions. They have heightened intuition which helps them with virtues of patience and intelligence, a true faithfulness to their beliefs and to others.

A soul incarnating on the blue ray has to learn boundaries with others, and to remember to take good care of their physical and emotional health. They have a tendency to work tirelessly, to martyr themselves for

others and the causes they believe in. Finding balance is a common life theme with people who feel so much. Being aware of energy drains and others who take advantage of their good nature is usually a lesson they learn early in life when someone else takes something cherished from them. As they mature they recognize the need to take control of their energetic environment on a different path from their own without becoming emotionally cold or distant.

In the ray of love and wisdom souls can often find difficulty in partnership and romantic matters if they find it too overwhelming to trust again once they have been betrayed. They have tendencies to mourn the loss of a partner longer and close their hearts to trying again when experiencing a lower thought process. A highly evolved soul learns how to heal from these events and to manifest the relationship which best compliments the life they desire to live. When living at the highest potential of the ray, these life themes are healed with intuitive guidance, patience and a miracle or two.

Awareness of a blue ray soul is also described as living the ray of applied consciousness. It is an incredible cohesion of creation and manifestation when operating at its highest vibration. When you recognize these qualities in yourself and in others, you know and appreciate how much they offer, and you create an amazing collaboration which raises the vibration of this planet.

(Published in OM Times Magazine)

18

RETURNING TO THE CONSCIOUSNESS OF PEACE

It can happen in moments of extreme gratitude or times of great chaos in our lives. The feeling when time ceases to exist and a radiant energy fills you from the inside. Your very soul is listening to what spirit has to say. Calmness surrounds you in celebration or rescue to let you know it really is going to be okay. You feel a peaceful calm taking over, guiding you through stormy waters and you want to stay there forever.

The inner self-talk of negativity melts away, replaced with a glowing love that is vibrant and alive. There is no allowing of fear in those moments and the connection that sustains you reaches you with an unshakable knowing. Your consciousness is bathing in peace. In those moments we have broken free from the illusion we are ever separated from this love which fills our hearts with peaceful thoughts. This amazing vibration has the ability to reach every atom of your being.

Imagine that someone on the other side of the world has the same kind of moment at the very same time. In synchronicity your souls touch in the spiritual consciousness and the spark ignites into a luminous energy. Two souls awaken to touch two more souls who heal and awaken. They can feel the vibration lifting them up into this peaceful existence, knowing this is how we were meant to evolve. A miraculous meeting of light minded people who sent out a beacon to find their resonating kindred spirits "out there."

All the human connections being made on Earth now through technological advances have changed our perceptions greatly. We can connect to each other in ways that were never possible before because of physical limitations. We understand better what happens on one side of this planet can greatly change the lives of the people who live on the other. It is truly incredible that one great thought can multiply into a thousand great thoughts through the consciousness that lives inside all of this human drama we must look through.

Even though there seems to be darkness and fear living in many people, remember it really only appears this way because these situations get the most attention. News media can make us feel this way by the constant reporting of doom and destruction. We must look at these situations and see how they can be healed instead of glorified or duplicated by those who are unaware. There are thousands of people coming into awareness. Their thoughts, actions and vibrations can help us to raise the frequency, transmuting the negative into positive outcomes and understanding for change.

There is a purpose to all this love and energy we share; whether to lift us higher or to help us heal. Our awakenings have happened simultaneously by reaching out in our new state of awareness. We are finding our kindred spirits, soul groups and purposes--learning to communicate in many ways and forms to help each other find our humanity with compassion for each other. We are opening up the portals that teach us why and how it matters. For those that need healing, the ripple effect across oceans of energy is being felt. We are rearranging our minds to leave behind old thought patterns of negativity that contain the past and things that no longer serve the greater good.

The sparkling beauty of peace is written in our DNA. The codes, keys and insights are blooming like flowers all around us if we look closely and tune in. The mysteries we seek to understand and the conditions we long to solve can no longer be hidden from us by our fear or indifference if we make the choice to be courageous. Remember that we came from a loving, breathing consciousness of peace that is very much alive. It is patiently waiting for us to reach out, touch it for ourselves and share it like the life sustaining miracle that it is.

From the Author:

I posted this article on my website blog in November of 2014. A few days later I received a profound and beautiful email from a man named Roger;

Good morning, Ms. Lynch,

This is just a note to thank you for your inspirational website which I had the joy of discovering this morning.

I am a retired Christian pastor from a conservative denomination which does not acknowledge or appreciate the lovely psychic gifts such as mediumship. Since my retirement two years ago I have become strongly attracted to mediumship and I have come to appreciate gifts such as yours. I want to learn as much as I can and I have been consulting the websites of metaphysical practitioners, spiritualists and mediums. Your website is truly enlightening and uplifting for me. Thank you so very much.

I especially appreciate your blog post article titled "Returning to the Consciousness of Peace." And one of the loveliest pieces of writing that I have read in the last few years is your statement that (please forgive me for quoting your words verbatim) " We were born to have hope. . . . Our mental perceptions of the Other Side and the Universe are coming into focus. Our senses are waking up to every possibility available to us through our endless creations in light and love." Thank you again.

I deeply regret the unfair judgments that some Christians often make about mediums.

Please accept my sincere compliments for your work and for your website.

Peace and Joy,

Roger

So, in closing, I want to thank you Roger for shining a light of inspiration and hope. I am ever grateful for your words.

ABOUT THE AUTHOR

Judi Lynch is a psychic medium, healing energy channel, spiritual adviser, teacher and writer. Contributing columnist for OM Times Magazine online and author of the book, Friends With Lights, A True Story. President of the Crystal Healing Foundation, Inc., a non-profit dedicated to healing.

www.psychicmediumjudilynch.com

www.jusilynch.com

www.crystalhealingspiritualcenter.com

I have worked with countless clients in the United States and around the world, been a featured guest on several radio shows and authored many spiritual and metaphysical articles. I teach workshops on psychic development and healing energy and I am currently working with others individually to heighten their abilities. Through study of the spiritual consciousness, vibrational energy channeling, ascension awareness and meditation, we can empower one another to heal and feel the joy life has to offer us. As more people awaken to find their spiritual selves coming alive, we need to reach out and help each other find the answers and comfort in these lives we are living here on Earth right now.

www.ingramcontent.com/pod-product-compliance
Lightning Source LLC
LaVergne TN
LVHW021613080426
835510LV00019B/2548